PRAISE FOR *THE CALL OF INTUITION*

"A beautiful and insightful book full of positivity, techniques, and ways to believe in yourself and trust your intuition."

: medium,
abri Tarot

"In this wonderful, easy-to   en shows
us how to connect to our   dom, and
inspiration through six simp.. ,..ucuces... The world needs more intuitive, empowered, and heart-centered warriors—this book is a practical guide and an important contribution toward that reality. I loved it—you will, too!"

—Beáta Alföldi, international retreat leader, medicine woman,
and author of *Shamanism in the New Millennium*

"With great warmth and wisdom, *The Call of Intuition* invites you on a journey into the multifaceted ways the intuitive self synthesizes information from our gut, heart, and mind to help guide and align us... Relatable, compassionate, and educated, Kris deftly draws on her own experience, her vast spiritual knowledge, and her keen insights for an enlightened read."

—Dr. BethAnne K. W., author of *Things of That Nature:
Words for the Mystic Heart*

"There is no better time than now to connect to that ever-liberating and empowering inner work that comes through the call of your intuition... Whether you are completely new to this type of work or you are ready to deepen your intuitive practice, this book will be your North Star in these challenging times."

—Jarka Kunova, business consultant and mentor

"One of the most important things that we can do individually and collectively as a species is move from our busy programmed minds to our heart-centered intuition. This book is the road map for us to do that. Thank you, Kris, for this timely piece of art and wisdom."

—Tom Cronin, leading meditation teacher and author of *The Portal*

The
CALL OF
INTUITION

ABOUT THE AUTHOR

Kris Franken is a spiritual author, teacher, and mentor. She is devoted to empowering others to live in deep alignment with their Soul's path and honor their intuition every step of the way. Her message of deeper connection, wilder love, and unbreakable self-trust has been shared with thousands of seekers all over the world.

Graduating with a bachelor's degree in psychology and sociology has given Kris an insatiable curiosity and intimate understanding of human behavior and intention. She is an eternal student of the intuitive arts and a humbled child of the universe.

Originally from Canada, Kris has lived in Detroit, Melbourne, and Sydney, and now gratefully calls Byron Bay—on Bundjalung land, Australia—home, sweet home.

KRIS FRANKEN

The

CALL OF
INTUITION

How to
Recognize & Honor
Your Intuition, Instinct
& Insight

LLEWELLYN PUBLICATIONS
Woodbury, Minnesota

First Edition
First Printing, 2020

Cover design by Shira Atakpu
Editing by Samantha Lu Sherratt
Interior chakra figure by Mary Ann Zapalac

Llewellyn Publications is a registered trademark of Llewellyn Worldwide Ltd.

Library of Congress Cataloging-in-Publication Data
Names: Franken, Kris, author.
Title: The call of intuition : how to recognize & honor your intuition, instinct & insight / Kris Franken.
Description: First edition. | Woodbury, Minnesota : Llewellyn Publications, [2020] | Includes bibliographical references and index.
Identifiers: LCCN 2020031291 (print) | LCCN 2020031292 (ebook) | ISBN 9780738765938 (paperback) | ISBN 9780738765983 (ebook)
Subjects: LCSH: Intuition. | Mindfulness (Psychology) | Meditation. | Self-actualization (Psychology)
Classification: LCC BF315.5 .F727 2020 (print) | LCC BF315.5 (ebook) | DDC 153.4/4—dc23
LC record available at https://lccn.loc.gov/2020031291
LC ebook record available at https://lccn.loc.gov/2020031292

Llewellyn Publications
A Division of Llewellyn Worldwide Ltd.
2143 Wooddale Drive
Woodbury, MN 55125-2989
www.llewellyn.com
Printed in the United States of America

DEDICATED TO THE WILD SOULS;
honor your heart and live free.

Contents

List of Practices and Rituals ... xi

Introduction: Welcome to the Wild Universe Within ... 1

PART ONE: THE INTUITIVE WAY

Chapter 1: Take a Look Inside Your Inner Wisdom ... 11

Chapter 2: Three Wise Inner Guides ... 19

Chapter 3: Alignment with Your Soul ... 45

PART TWO: SIX STEPS FOR THRIVING INTUITIVELY

Chapter 4: Breathe ... 59

Chapter 5: Surrender ... 77

Chapter 6: Connect ... 111

Chapter 7: Trust ... 161

Chapter 8: Honor ... 179

Chapter 9: Nourish ... 195

Conclusion and Appreciation ... 223

Acknowledgments ... 225

Bibliography ... 229

Recommended Resources ... 233

Index ... 235

Practices

Love and Light Soul Prompts ... 14

Self-Aware Soul Prompts ... 17

Gut Instinct Soul Prompts ... 27

Heart-Led Intuition Soul Prompts ... 37

Mind's Insight Soul Prompts ... 43

Deep Breathing Soul Prompts ... 67

Whole Awareness Soul Prompts ... 73

Releasing Attachments Soul Prompts ... 80

Space Clearing Soul Prompts ... 94

Mindful Magic Soul Prompts ... 100

Complete Surrender Soul Prompts ... 109

Self-Connection Soul Prompts ... 119

Wild Energy Soul Prompts ... 134

Serendipity Soul Prompts ... 152

Create Your Own Reading ... 158

Self-Trust Soul Prompts ... 173

Authentic Wisdom Soul Prompts ... 180

Inspired Morning Questions ... 183

Contemplative Evening Questions ... 184

Quirky and Gifted Soul Prompts ... 192

Sacred Self-Care Soul Prompts ... 202

Shadow Self Soul Prompts ... 204

Rituals

Alignment Meditation ... 53

Box Breathing Exercise ... 65

Affirmations for the Breath ... 71

A Spirited Prayer ... 74

A Prayer of Release ... 83

Sunrise Prayer for Surrender ... 101

Mother Earth Meditation ... 102

Create a Sacred Altar ... 103

Colorful Therapy ... 103

Morning Love Visualization ... 105

Weekly Clearing Visualization ... 106

Affirmations for Surrender ... 108

Insightful Meditation ... 112

Intuitive Meditation ... 114

Instinctive Meditation ... 115

Mother Earth Visualization ... 128

Spirit Guide Connection Meditation ... 138

Angel Connection Meditation ... 142

Connection with Loved Ones Meditation ... 145

Discover Your Psychic Gifts Meditation ... 154

Affirmations for Self-Empowerment ... 169

Intuitive Muscle Testing ... 175

Affirmations for Gratitude ... 193

Everyday Self-Love Affirmations ... 198

Wild Energy Revivers ... 209

Nourish Your Inner Cosmos ... 212

A Prayer for Your Soul's Voyage ... 224

WELCOME TO THE
WILD UNIVERSE WITHIN

Your inner world is a creative, expressive, and deeply intelligent universe, providing you with guidance in each moment of the day. Think of each biological system as a galaxy, each organ as a planet, and each breath as a circulation of the sacred lifeforce that nourishes the whole. Imagine your gut instinct is like the moon, moving in cycles—some days feeling so potent and powerful, other days almost out of reach, but always there, orbiting and creating an inner foundation as you walk your Soul's wild path. Picture your intuitive heart as a sun—a warm and constant presence, the center of your inner universe—keeping you sustained, guided, loved, and flawlessly in tune with the present moment. Imagine the psychic insights that fall into your mind as stars—some brighter than others, all of them precious celestial bodies of information—sparking the light within you as they open you to new thoughts, ideas, and awareness.

This is the universe within, the unlimited magic of your being. As you grow in intuitive self-awareness, you'll get to know intimately the untamed wisdom of your heart, the inconceivable strength of your Soul, the sensual intelligence of your body, and the brilliant complexity of your mind.

What does it mean to be *called* by your intuition? It means to gently and consistently pay conscious attention to your inner intelligence and be guided by it. That's what this book is all about. The wise world within you is calling to you in every moment; it's up to you to make the connection, listen, and honor it.

Living according to the call of intuition is both liberating and empowering. It asks you to surrender what isn't meant for you and trust what is. It calls you to give up the need to control life and embrace the act of co-creation. It's finding flow where there was once force. It's seeking truth over perfection or being right. It's allowing the wordless, loving wisdom within to guide you along your journey. Honestly, it's an imperfect, messy, unmapped route, but, all the same, it's wildly magnificent, fulfilling, abundant, and worthwhile.

As your intuitive heart moves you forward toward what's best for you, your instinctive gut is pulling you away from what isn't aligned with your highest good, and your insightful brain is opening to creative wisdom. These three wisdom guides—instinct, intuition, and insight—have a unique place in your body, mind, and spirit. Knowing how they guide you in their distinct ways will bring a powerful new depth to your self-awareness. And while your wisdom may *seem* invisible, know with certainty that it's alive, tangible, present, and accessible within your being.

THE UNFOLDING OF THIS BOOK

I've been curious about self-empowerment my whole life. As a highly intuitive and stubbornly independent being, I've made it my quest to learn from countless teachers how to live my truth in ways that resonate with my Soul. I've sat with shamanic practitioners, learned from a range of spiritual guides, found potent transformation with holistic healers, witnessed past life regressions, and journeyed to the astral plane. I've connected with many psychics, seers, and intuitives, learned to channel information from Spirit in my own way, studied the chakra system and taught others to heal their chakras, connected with my Canadian indigenous ancestors, healed the deepest parts of my shadow self, and empowered myself with as much spiritual knowledge as I could carry. I share this with you so that you will know how deeply I've opened to spiritual work and held *nothing* back in the process, and as a result I have considerable experience and compassion to draw on as I guide you toward your own inner transformation.

As a wellness and spirituality writer with over fourteen years' experience, I've infused this experience into hundreds of articles for *Cosmopolitan*, *Grazia*, *Collective Hub*, *Good Health*, *body+soul*, *Real Living*, *Thrive Global*, and many other print and online magazines. I enjoy researching a subject until I am so familiar with the idea that it comes to life within me.

I'm blessed to be a psychic clairvoyant medium. That means I receive insights from Spirit, mostly through my inner senses of sight and hearing; plus, I get to chat to Loved Ones who have passed on. Around the time I turned forty, I realized I had proficient psychic skills that I could use to help others who were feeling stuck, confused, or lost—especially those who were craving more purpose in life. I honed these skills with various mentors before offering oracle and tarot readings to friends and eventually expanding to clients all over the world. I also offer Soul purpose mentorships to those who desire more clarity and alignment with their purpose. I'm a meditation teacher—I guide clients through meditations to help clear blocks, I record meditations for Insight Timer, and I guide circles and groups through healing and inspiring meditations. I'm also a certified Reiki I and II healer, which has widened my understanding of the nature of energy: how it moves, heals, transforms, and transmutes.

The beautiful and unexpected emergence of the central ideas in this book came to me in a moment of insight that I can't quite fathom but will never forget. One afternoon, a few months after I began to deeply explore the inner world of intuition, I was sitting at my beloved writing desk, musing about intuition on social media. I was being creative and, not wanting to sound repetitive, using various words to mean the same as intuition, such as *instinct*, *sixth sense*, and *third eye*. After I finished, I began to read the musings out loud to myself, then halfway through, I stopped. A knowing came from my body, a deep understanding arose, and I suddenly knew with magnificent clarity that my gut instinct, wholehearted intuition, and psychic insight were three completely different ways of expressing the wisdom within. The difference between them was palpable; I could feel their energy swirl inside me.

It took a mountain of research to understand this in such a way that I could easily pass on to others. My mind opened with endless curiosity, asking questions such as these: What did each of them do? Did they sound different? Were they tangible? Where did they come from? How could I make the inner voices clearer?

It excited me enormously, this new way of understanding inner wisdom. I was eager to experiment on myself to discover if what was revealing itself was effective in the real world. Amazingly, everything I discovered—either through books mentioned in the bibliography or through spontaneous and spirited insight—felt undeniably substantial and vivid.

In the moment, the wise world within looked like three pulsing lights—bursting with information and love—within the body: one in the belly, another in the chest, and the third in the brain. The fiery hearth, the effusive heart, and the receptive head. The belly pulsed with grounded wisdom, the chest with expansive guidance, and the brain with spirited connection. The more I researched, the more these lights unfolded and guided me toward the most astonishing understanding of my inner universe.

As much as I poured endless devotion from my mind, heart, and spirit onto these pages, I believe the credit for this book belongs to the angel or muse who dropped that staggering wisdom onto my lap that day. I'm grateful for the life-changing portal into deeper self-awareness that I'm delighted to illuminate for you here.

WHAT'S TUCKED INSIDE THESE PAGES

As a mentor, psychic, and teacher, I'm fortunate to assist many clients intuitively along their spiritual paths. As I hold space for their growth and transformation, I discover what prevents them from listening to and trusting their wisdom. Once these blocks are surrendered and healed, I've seen how people come to life when they are finally able to trust and honor their Soul-deep yearnings. This is an important part of my purpose; I am deeply honored to do this work for others. This work has greatly shaped this book and ensured that what I share here assists people in everyday, real-life situations.

Part one of this book is a comprehensive and fresh look at inner wisdom and how it comes to life in your being. Each wisdom guide (instinct, intuition, and insight) consistently receives information from within and around you to provide guidance each moment of the day. All three work independently and yet so seamlessly together. Understanding the inherent nature of your guides is essential for the deepest possible experience of you as you live life to the fullest.

Even though intuition is just one part of the whole, along with instinct and insight, you'll find in this book that I accentuate the importance of living intuitively. Your instinct will protect you. Insights will find you. But it's your intuition that guides you toward a life of truth, magic, and bliss. It's your intuition that you must *deliberately* follow if you're going to have the greatest chance of living a fulfilled life.

Part two of this book is a six-step process to confidently learn to live from an empowered state of self-awareness. This process will show you how to consciously breathe, surrender, connect, trust, honor, and nourish your way to a deeper relationship with yourself. It's a fluid practice that you can take with you everywhere you go—a way to understand and open yourself fully to the guidance within.

The heart-centered ideas on these pages are grounded in some of the most awe-inspiring science, giving you a modern understanding of the ancient wisdom that runs through your veins, your energy field, your breath, your neural pathways, and beyond.

All the subtle and profound insights I've learned along my personal journey, the rituals and habits I've put into practice, the easy and uncomfortable steps along my path, the sublime spirituality and the astonishing science, and everything else that has strengthened my connection to my intuitive self in some way are here on these pages.

ADVICE FROM MY HEART AS YOU BEGIN YOUR JOURNEY

Getting to know your true self is a lifetime's work. Some days it's the rockiest path; other days it's sweet serendipity. There may be people in your life who won't encourage you to honor your inner wisdom, sacred lifeforce, brave magic, or audacious dreams. Do it anyway with all of your heart. Most of us are encouraged to work hard, think logically, and look outside of ourselves for the answers. All around us are so many choices, directions, ideas, and experts who say they know what's best for us. But we've forgotten that we *already know*.

The number one regret of the dying, as noted by Bronnie Ware in her book *The Top Five Regrets of the Dying*, is that they wish they'd had the courage to live a life true to themselves, not the life others expected of them.[1] Trust yourself, sweet ancient Soul. Trust that you have all the wisdom and answers inside your heart. Trust that you know what's right for you. Trust that you know the way. Trust that everything in your life has led you perfectly to this place.

To bring your experiences to life while reading this book, I recommend using an accompanying notebook to explore the Soul prompts and other exercises. The more you fully participate in the processes within this book, the more they will resonate within every aspect of your life. Take notes on your journey with consistency, honesty, and vulnerability. If what you've shared in writing feels too raw to leave unattended in a journal, rip out and safely burn the pages when you're done.

The meditations in this book are a powerful way to go beyond the words and feel into the unseen world. There is no perfect way to meditate, so go with what works for you. Make sure you're comfortable, keep an open mind, and stay fluid. If you ever feel uncomfortable during a meditation, simply say, "I ask that only beings of unconditional love and light be with me now and clear the energy within and around me of all that is not of my being or for my highest good." When you have finished with a prayer, say, "And so it is," so that you feel and know that it has already been answered for your highest possible good. For at least thirty minutes after a potent meditation, avoid all screens and busy social situations as they can interfere with your connection, sense of peace, and high vibration. You may be teary, serene, delicate, or powerfully emotional; sit with this. Let the emotions flow. Move slowly

1. Ware, *The Top Five Regrets of the Dying*, 37.

back into the world. Eat a healthy snack, walk barefoot on grass, have a shower or bath, or intuitively stretch your body to ground yourself.

A NOTE OF GRATITUDE

In this book, you'll meet yourself safely, powerfully, lovingly, and in a way that will help you live from your truth with deeper courage and compassion. By the end, you will know without a doubt what your wisdom sounds like, where it comes from, why your inner guides are your most trusted advisors and companions, and how to bring your own guidance to life in the most vivid and uninhibited ways.

The world needs more intuitive, self-aware warriors. Thank you for heeding your Soul's call. Now let's fall head over heels into the wild universe within.

—Kris

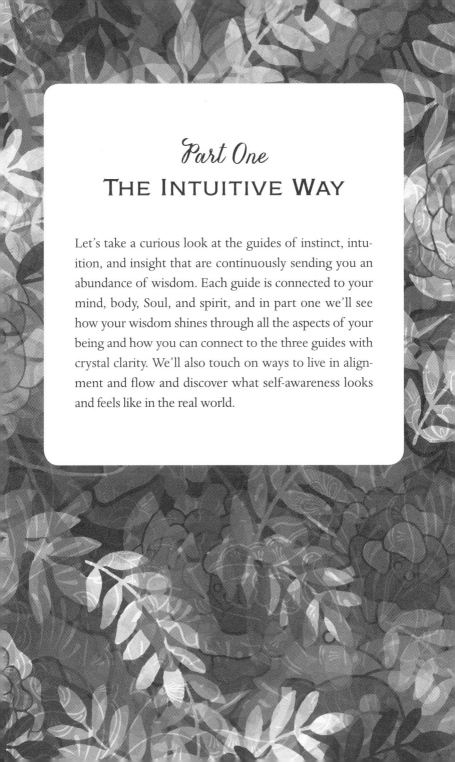

Part One
THE INTUITIVE WAY

Let's take a curious look at the guides of instinct, intuition, and insight that are continuously sending you an abundance of wisdom. Each guide is connected to your mind, body, Soul, and spirit, and in part one we'll see how your wisdom shines through all the aspects of your being and how you can connect to the three guides with crystal clarity. We'll also touch on ways to live in alignment and flow and discover what self-awareness looks and feels like in the real world.

TAKE A LOOK INSIDE
YOUR INNER WISDOM

"You always know. You've always known. You'll always know."
—GURU JAGAT

You are so wise.

You are a spiritual being of light with infinite access to your inner well of guidance anytime you need it. Your instinct, intuition, and insight are already within you. Right this moment, your being is bursting with love and wisdom, guidance and gentleness, radical ideas and wild creativity, solutions and answers, protection and nurturing. Physically, energetically, spiritually, and mentally, your inner intelligence is well and truly alive. Oh, you are *so wise.* This intelligence doesn't need to be found or created; it's the awareness of and connection to your inner self that can be strengthened. The stronger the connection, the more obvious the guidance will be.

Your unique intelligence is the most loving, sovereign, and accurate guiding force you'll ever find. It's always with you, waiting for you to open up to it and listen. It's such an intrinsic, tangible, and visceral part of who you are.

Life can be distracting, hectic, overwhelming, daunting, exhausting, and fast. Your inner compass, however, is still, all-knowing, serene, and content. When you slow down enough to listen to your inner world, you'll navigate the outer world with deeper presence, ease, and grace.

So ... *listen.*

In the beginning, you'll tap into your wisdom occasionally—like when you're finding a comfortable place to sit on a bus, choosing a fresh juice that nourishes your body, journaling your raw thoughts on a situation, doing a heart-led meditation, or shopping for groceries that nourish your body's unique needs. It may come and go in bursts. You'll understand "coincidences," you'll remember vivid dreams and sense what they mean, you'll experience and welcome extraordinary insight, you'll feel wisdom direct from your body, and you'll begin to recognize your inner voice as a consistent pull toward truth and alignment. After a while, these moments will occur more regularly, and you'll live more often than not in communion with your spirit.

However your precious inner connection grows, accept and nurture it. Allow it to open up and expand into all areas of your life. Tune in often and watch your life flourish.

THE ESSENTIAL QUALITIES OF INSTINCT, INTUITION, AND INSIGHT

Your inner voice is subtle, positive, consistent, and peaceful; it springs to life when you pay attention to it, when you show gratitude and trust what's coming through. This voice helps with big decisions around your career, relationships, parenting, health, and finances; it also guides the small choices that fill your day, such as choosing an outfit, planning meals, shopping, conversations, traveling, exercises, journaling, social media, friends, and entertainment.

The essence of your instinct is grounded security; it wants to take care of you each day and keep you safe. The essence of your intuition is heart-opening expansion; it wants to open you up to love and limitless living. The essence of your insight is inspiring new information that comes to you as you open your mind to the universe around you. Quite often, these guides work together to guide you fluidly along your path. When you receive this inner guidance, you'll know it's from your collective wise inner voice (and not your ego) if it has these three key features:

It's from love.
Your inner guidance is always loving and kind, confident and sure, compassionate and gentle, soothing and calm. It's never sarcastic, dramatic, negative, or fearful. It's not trying to play games with you, nor is it changing its mind every few minutes. That's your ego. While your journey may often feel unpredictable, your inner wisdom will be a source of loving consistency every single day. You may feel challenged because it's taking you out of your comfort zone, but it only wants you to fulfill your highest potential.

It's you.
Your personal wisdom should feel familiar, safe, and just like home. It knows your deepest needs and has your best interests at heart. It's not the ego's echoes of your parents, teachers, bullies, or friends—it's the voice of your honest self, your whole self, the real you.

It feels true.
You'll know that you're aligned with the truth of your deepest wisdom when your body feels light and expansive. You'll know when something isn't right for you because you'll feel constricted, awkward, fidgety, tense, or edgy. Physical sensations of inner truth

vary from person to person; you'll have your own signature sensations guiding you each moment.

· PRACTICE ·

Love and Light Soul Prompts

Take a moment to become familiar with how your own wisdom sounds. You could try answering these prompts with a pen and journal, or you could simply meditate on them.

What does love want you to know right now? If you tune in to the feeling of divine self-love, are there any messages that come through? If you don't receive messages of words, are there any sensations that you feel? What is your experience like?

With one hand on your heart, speak to your heart like it's a friend: a wise companion who knows intimately your Soul's important path. If you're not sure what to say, begin with a few words of gratitude for the way it intuitively guides you. How does it feel to talk to your heart?

What would it feel like to align with your Highest Self (the eternal part of you, your complete Soul)? Think back to the last time your life felt truly good: Were you content, happy, at ease, peaceful, energized, focused, or free? How would you describe that sense of alignment, as though you were living your best life?

What truth is opening up in your life that you cannot dismiss any longer? What do you need to do to acknowledge the wisdom already held in your heart? What is one step you'll take this week to honor your heart's wisdom?

Who or what makes you feel lit up and light? Who or what makes you feel stuck and heavy? Are there any actions that need to be put into place or conversations that need to be had around these feelings?

What does a self-aware life look like to you? Describe this in detail. Imagine it vividly. Bring it to life any way you wish on your journal pages or while meditating. Allow this to manifest in your world by stepping into it daily and doing one or two things that help shape this self-aware life you're creating. If self-awareness means journaling regularly, then create a space that makes journaling easy and enjoyable. If it means starting the day with meditation, then set an alarm that wakes you gently each morning. If it means lavishing yourself with intuitive self-care, then find a way to bring this into each day.

What It Means to Live a Self-Aware Life

When it comes to living intuitively, don't overthink it. It's simple, really. The ego wants to distract you and complicate it. If you can see past this daily deception, past your fears and outdated beliefs, you can see how pure and uncomplicated living from within genuinely is. Here are the main concepts:

Serendipity. Intuitive living means being open to and aware of *synchronicities*. When you're strongly connected to your inner world, life flows smoothly, and you manifest what you think about faster. Like when a friend calls just as you're thinking of them. Or when you pick up a book on a whim that has powerful advice for your current situation. It's the inkling that tells you what your kids, pets, family, or friends need when they're sick or stuck. It's the "random" conversation that leads to a "chance" meeting that develops into a new career, relationship, or healing path. It's one sweetly serendipitous moment after the other. When you're aligned with your Soul, you're aligned with the whole.

Alignment. Living consciously means living in *alignment* with what's true for you. Alignment is fluid communication from and connection with your Soul, your highest truth. Alignment is a vibration, a movement of energy that feels at once grounded, centered, and enlightened and propels you gracefully forward toward what feels good and meant for you.

Communion. Living with self-awareness means living in *communion* with yourself. Communion is a consistent state of kind and conscious connection with your body, emotions, energy, and surroundings. This begins with occasionally checking in on yourself, asking questions such as, "How am I today? How did that make me feel? What do I need now?" Through journaling, meditating, and cultivating mindfulness, a curious and empowering communication builds up until the connections flow together. This feels like an unbreakable, ongoing communion with self.

Self-care. Self-awareness means prioritizing your *well-being* and trusting that you know what's best for you. Be curious and get advice from a whole realm of holistic healers, but only follow the advice that feels true for you. And always ensure you're setting healthy boundaries.

Consciousness. Living *consciously* means being responsible and compassionate. Taking full responsibility for your life is so profoundly empowering and being compassionate toward yourself and others powerfully opens you up to the deepest joy and connection possible. Being conscious also means never holding on to an opinion too tightly while staying open to new ideas.

Rebellion. Often, intuitive living is about *going against the grain*; being at odds with society, friends, and family; and dropping expectations and old patterns of behavior. As a child, you were given road maps from your caregivers, teachers, and peers. Initially, these would have been helpful as you found your way, but if you don't spend time tuning in to your own inner guidance as an adult, you'll end up with confusing, crumpled-up bits of other people's weathered maps in your head—none of it making any good sense to you and the mileage you're currently traversing. Rip up the maps. Burn them. Let them fly. Give thanks for all the well-meaning advice you've been given. Start afresh. Go against what you've been taught if you need to. It may feel uncomfortable, but that's only because it's new.

Truth. Finally, honest awareness is only ever about *truth*, not perfection. Perfection is an illusion; it simply doesn't exist. Cease pursuing it, and you'll be free to follow your unique truth. Sometimes your truth will feel unexpected or unusual, but as long as it sounds like love and feels like home, it's the safest place to be.

· PRACTICE ·
Self-Aware Soul Prompts

Sit comfortably, take a deep breath, and consider these questions with a loving curiosity and with absolutely no judgment. Put pen to paper or perhaps share with a friend and have a conversation using these questions as prompts.

How does serendipity feel to you? Can you remember a day when everything fell into place beautifully, fortuitously, and without any major planning? How did that feel? Did you trust in the divine process, did you consider yourself lucky, or did you simply believe that life was on your side? How can you allow for more serendipity in your life?

What does alignment mean to you? How do you find flow in your life? What feels out of alignment at the moment? What is causing your energy to feel off-center, and how does your heart—the center of your being—desire to bring you back into a calm and aligned state?

How do you feel today? Do you take care of yourself? Can you create a healthy celebration ritual at the end of each day that feels like closure and joy, such as lighting a candle or writing down what you're grateful for?

How can you be more responsible in your life in order to empower yourself fully? Are there conversations you need to have or changes that need to be made to feel truly empowered and wholly responsible? What needs to be changed that you are resisting? Where is the resistance coming from and how can you dissolve it so that necessary and heartfelt change can be made?

What expectations are you feeling called to rebel against? In what ways are you living according to what other people or society expects of you? How can you step away from this into your truth? How can you express your hidden desires so that the life you lead is all from your heart? How can you create quiet space to hear your rebellious voice?

How can you see through the desire for perfection and find the truth in any situation? Perfection is a state we can never reach; honesty and peace are higher states worth pursuing. Where can you let go of perfection today? How can you embrace a blissfully messy life for the sake of peace?

Chapter 2
THREE WISE INNER GUIDES

"You are beginning to understand, aren't you?
That the whole world is inside you:
in your perspectives and in your heart."
—UNKNOWN

In this chapter, we'll be looking at the three inner guides that influence and inform you. We'll start with ancient gut instinct. Next, we'll look at wholehearted intuition, then we'll get into inspiring insight. Following that, we'll discover the importance of alignment and flow when living within this kind of self-awareness and how to move into a state of inner harmony with ease.

GUIDE 1: INSTINCT

The role of your gut instinct is to keep you safe in every area of your life and to help you avoid what is not aligned with your highest truth. It's the protective energy in and around your belly that is formed within your unconscious mind, your physical gut, and the primal spirit of this area. Instinct works on such an unseen level and is taken for granted because we rarely consciously access what's in there. However, when you get to know how your instinct works, you can heal and nourish it to feel grounded and safe.

Evolution of Instinct

Your instinct lives in your gut, which is connected physically and energetically to the reptilian brain. The reptilian brain, located at the central base of the brain, controls the body's primal and vital functions such as heart rate, breathing, body temperature, balance, and self-preserving behavior patterns. This part of the brain is automatic, compulsive, and innate, and it keeps you alive through your well-formed instinct that constantly and unconsciously monitors the environment around you.

Your gut instinct has been part of you since the moment you were conceived, but its roots are ancient. Your instinct contains all the mastery for staying alive that your ancestors have accumulated since the emergence of the human species. In general, every single human being possesses the same general instinctive behaviors, but due to fluctuations along bloodlines—where familial instinct is honed—you will express them in different ways. In other words, your family history shapes your inherited instinct in subtle but powerful ways. If you never feel completely safe, it may be because your ancestors lived through war. If you always feel safe and grounded, you may have come from family who lived simpler lives connected to the land. There's so much more to it than this, and there are many reasons why your instinct has a particular way of influencing you.

As you can imagine, your childhood also shapes your instinct. Whether you were taught to fear hell or spiders, experienced traumatic or intense situations (and possibly forgot or repressed them), or were taught about how uncertain the world is—all the early beliefs you created have an impact on your instinct.

Everything positive you experienced as a child also makes a difference. Deep feelings of love, worthiness, safety, security, and belonging give your instinct a healthy foundation. Whatever your childhood looked like, it will generously color your impulses, reactions, urges, and beliefs that subtly but powerfully direct your life. The more you heal your past, family line, beliefs, and body, and the more you create ways to feel safe and secure, the more effective and grounded your instinct will be.

When in a healthy state, your instinct is loving, practical, useful, helpful, lifesaving, grounding, and informative. If it's unbalanced, it may feel like you're never safe, you don't belong, life is difficult to process, or you're not worthy enough. There are many ways to heal these imbalances, which we'll get to later on.

Unconscious Mind

The mind as a whole is made up of three layers: conscious, subconscious, and unconscious. Each works closely with your inner guides. The "mind" is described in many ways: as an unlimited field of information located in and beyond your brain, as the consciousness in each of your cells, or as the center of your experiences and interactions with the world. The brain, heart, and gut are also thought of as being the three "minds" of your being.

However your mind works and wherever it lives, it's good to at least understand the three layers and how they relate to each of your inner guides. Think of your mind as an iceberg with your unconscious mind—the largest part by far—as the section underwater (under consciousness), while the subconscious is the majority of the ice above the water, and the conscious mind is the tip of the iceberg.

The conscious mind is aware of anything you consciously direct your attention to. The subconscious mind holds information that you can easily recall. And the unconscious mind is packed full of life experiences and information that you cannot remember.

The unconscious mind is deeply connected to your instinct. Psychologists have discovered that this part of your mind is the underground warehouse of all your past experiences that have been forgotten or repressed. You can't consciously access your unconscious mind right now—there's no way to see what's in there while in your normal, day-to-day conscious state—but it's an important and impactful part of your mind. It's where your automatic responses, deep beliefs, unthinking habits, and instinctive behaviors come from. It's the foundation of your entire mind, even though you don't consciously know what's in there.

The ego comes from your personal instinct. The ego is a culmination of the fear-based voices of the caregivers, elders, teachers, and peers of your childhood. It loves to dominate, control, judge, complain, argue, and enforce the false idea of smallness (the opposite of your Highest Self) and separateness (the opposite of oneness). When you become conscious of your ego from the loving spaciousness of your Soul's perspective, it loses its power, which wasn't real anyway. It never disappears, but as you grow into a more peaceful and inclusive way of being, you're free to live according to love.

With curiosity and devotion to growth, you can nourish your instinct by bringing awareness and healing to your unconscious mind. Automatic writing, journaling, meditation, breathwork, and many forms of movement and exercise can help shift stuck unconscious energy or emotions, thoughts, and beliefs. We'll take a look at these exercises in the second part of the book.

Once you've finished this book, if you still feel like you have parts of your unconscious mind, outdated beliefs, your shadow side, or instincts to heal, I recommend finding a healer who can go deep with you in person. I've personally found immeasurable healing from psychologists who practice hypnosis or eye movement desensitization and reprocessing (EMDR), homeopaths who pair counseling with powerfully healing remedies, chiropractors who use neuro-emotional technique (NET), quantum kinesiologists, and shamanic healers who use ancient healing methods to traverse into your underworld and bring light to the shadows within.

When you understand the hidden, unconscious parts of yourself, you'll discover how you have always been driven by what you cannot see, and how ultimately you *can* connect deeply within to feel deeper peace and listen with ease to the protective voice of your instinct.

Gut Center

Your gut is the physical core of your instinct, as it (as well as your brain and heart) houses countless neurons (brain cells), which shows that it has a real intelligence. Your gut, brain, and heart actually each have a mind of their own, and they're all linked to each other by the vagus nerve. This nerve is the longest and most complex cranial nerve that connects the brain with the heart, gut, other organs, and beyond into your blood vessels. It carries information both ways—from the brain down to the lower organs and back up again—in a flash. It's what I call the *parasympathetic scenic route*, because when it's switched on—through meditation, deep breaths, yoga, chanting, or humming—you're in rest-and-digest mode. You feel at ease, mindful, grounded, and able to connect with a peaceful way of *being*. When you are calm, your organs, including your gut, are able to send positive, healing messages to your brain, which naturally influence the instructions that the brain gives to the body as a whole.

When you're stressed, you jump out of this way of being and into what I call the *sympathetic highway*. When your sympathetic nervous system is switched on, you're in fight-or-flight mode.

Stress, traffic, screens, poor sleep, an unhealthy diet, and many other factors contribute to this survival response in the body. This rushed and frenetic way of *doing* is not conducive to living mindfully as it throws you deep into your fear-driven thoughts and the chaos and turbulence of the external world. It puts you on edge and prepares you (usually unnecessarily) for danger, which makes it harder, if not impossible, to tune in to your inner world.

As it goes, you're either in one state or the other. When you actively relax your body, you're strengthening your connection to your inner wisdom by nourishing your vagus nerve. When you unconsciously or purposefully search out or create stress in your life to get an adrenalin hit, you're denying and blocking yourself from your own truth that yearns to be heard.

The sensations of your gut instinct can be feeling sick, nauseous, or squeamish, indicating that whatever you're faced with has the potential to make you unwell, be it outdated food, plane turbulence, or a mouse in the kitchen. Sometimes you'll feel off or wary, but there won't be any obvious reason for this. Energetically, this is your instinct working on a subtler realm, informing you of a harmful or misaligned object, person, or situation that you might not be consciously aware of.

Researchers have discovered powerful communication from the gut to the brain that indicates our instinct is strongly linked to the gut.[2] In an interesting review of the way the gut communicates with the brain, it was noted that signals along the vagus nerve from the gastrointestinal tract act as a red flag by cutting off the reward systems in the brain so that we're directed to avoid dangerous situations. In other words, physical feedback from the gut to

2. Maniscalco and Rinaman, "Vagal Interoceptive Modulation of Motivated Behavior," 151–167.

the brain is protective and encourages us to be cautious whenever anything potentially harmful is near.

This is another reason why it pays to meditate or do yoga regularly. When your vagus nerve is healthy and communicating freely and fluidly, it can easily guide your brain so that you are likely to steer clear of whatever isn't right for you.

Your instinct also generates automatic and reflexive responses. When you burn your finger, you swiftly remove your hand from the source of heat before your mind is aware of what happened. You might see the shadow of a bird about to swoop and duck your head instinctively. Your foot may hit the brakes of your car before you can see another car pull in front of you without a signal. Your five senses feed your instinct constantly so that you can react instantaneously.

Physical and emotional gut-centered healing has endless benefits that go beyond healthy digestive function. If the physical gut is out of balance, your instinct may be overly fearful, unnaturally sensitive, or stuck in past issues or trauma, which may numb or fragment its power, alertness, and ability to keep you grounded and feeling safe. Looking at it from a different angle, when healing fears or past traumas, you're strengthening the gut function and related instinctive communication.

Take care of your gut. Eat intuitively. Breathe deeply. Nourish yourself.

Primal Spirit

You are your Soul, the watcher, the oldest and wisest part of you. At your core, you are the eternal energetic presence of love and light, the nonphysical being that transcends time and space.

Your Soul is the spiritual guidance center that works with your mind, body, and spirit. Your enduring spirit is the energetic expression of your Soul that influences your mind and body. Your spirit is part of the unseen energetic matrix. We often describe energy as something we *have* rather than something we *are*. We are all energetic beings, as is everything around us. *Everything*. Everything that looks alive, solid, or empty is all energy. Anything that is alive—people, animals, trees, plants, flowers, crystals, rocks, earth, water, food—has an energetic presence emanating from its Soul called its spirit.

Your thoughts, emotions, speech, and activities all have their own energy and will affect how your spirit as a whole vibrates and, therefore, how you feel energetically. When your spirit is light and sparkly or dense and murky, it's no accident; you caused it to be that way. And it will without a doubt affect everything within and around you.

What we're learning now through science is what the intuitive teachers and mystics have always taught about energy: we live in an energetic matrix where our inner experience affects the waves of energy all around us, and the waves of energy around us have the potential to affect our inner experience as well. Everything is connected, and everything we think, believe, say, or do matters and makes a difference.

There is a sacred essence to your instinct, a swirling of energy that is out of your conscious reach. The effect you have on others, the way you manifest in your life, the blocks that are in the way of happiness, and the repetitive nature of your relationships, habits, complaints, and blessings are all directed by the energy created from your unconscious mind.

To heal your unconscious beliefs and programs is to heal the energy that charges your instinct. This opens you up to your unlimited potential; without the ego's commentary and the shadows of survival tripping your every step, you are liberated in your pursuit of purpose, abundance, satisfaction, and love.

The scientific understanding of your energy focuses on the electromagnetic field (EMF) around your body. Each organ, including the stomach, has an EMF. The EMF around your gut extends out into the lower vibrations of your environment to discern if you're safe, and, if not, what is interfering with your safety. This could be anything from an unsafe dark street to an ill-intentioned animal, an unsteady bridge, a storm brewing, an energy vampire amongst your friends, or a misaligned career move.

Your mysterious and age-old instinct is a master teacher in your life. As you heal the deepest parts of you, it will guide you ever more powerfully.

· PRACTICE ·
Gut Instinct Soul Prompts

Let's take a look at your incredible gut instinct. There are so many wild and wondrous ways it wants to guide and protect you. As you journal with these (if you don't have a pen and paper, simply take a languid moment to contemplate them), let yourself be patient, honest, and raw. If you edit or hold back, you may not get to the gold of your instinct's hidden wisdom.

What does your gut feel like when it's telling you to stay away from a person, place, situation, or idea? Is it tight, restrictive, nauseous, or otherwise unsettled? If you ask your gut to show you directly what "no" or "keep clear" feels like, how does it respond?

How does your physical gut need healing, and what will you do to nourish it? If it feels tight from stress, you could look for ways to actively bring peace or closure to the root cause of your tension. If it feels unhappy from particular foods, you might enjoy lighter or different foods for a while. If it feels ignored, try connecting with it gently to soothe and understand it better. If it feels uneasy, is there a message for you to look into?

What unconscious beliefs do you think might be driving your everyday actions? You may not know consciously or precisely what they are, but you can use your gut sensations to guide you as you work through these questions. What were you taught as a child about money, success, friendships, relationships, sex, religion, nature, exercise, your body, food, and health? How have these beliefs stayed with you in subtle or strong ways? Even noticing this can have a restorative ripple effect. Don't judge what comes up— just witness it, and if you don't like what you notice, set an intention to let it go and replace it with a more empowering belief.

How has your instinct protected you? Where has it asked you to change direction? Can you recall a time recently when you cancelled an appointment, changed your plans, or drove a different route? Was that decision from an inner feeling? If so, describe the moment in detail; this will provide you with a precious understanding of how your personal instinct works.

What ancestors are you particularly grateful for when it comes to laying a secure foundation for your instinct? Are there any ancestors whose legacy you would like to forgive and heal? If you don't know much about your ancestors, ask family members for their stories and get to know how they lived. You can also look up your ancestors online to find out more about who they were or where they came from, or connect to a recommended psychic medium.

Guide 2: Intuition

Your powerful intuition is a unique blend of energetic feedback, physical awareness, memories and experience, and messages from Spirit. It's so much more than a good guess. It's *real* and not as elusive as you might think. It works by tuning in to the awareness and feedback from your physical heart and energetic heartspace, your subconscious mind, and your spirit, which all inform you without the need for conscious reasoning. It's the wholehearted knowing that has been guiding you your whole life, and now you get to open up to it more intimately.

Development of Intuition

The limbic brain, located above the reptilian brain and surrounded by the neocortex, is related to intuition and was the second part of our brain to develop as a species. The limbic brain is important for many reasons—mainly that it remembers behaviors that either feel good or bad—and it's responsible for your subconscious emotions, memories, and physical senses. All these elements are crucial to the development and expression of your intuition.

While the instinct guides by restriction, your intuition guides by expansion. Intuition is based on love instead of fear, connection over competition, creativity instead of predictability, and consideration rather than reflexes.

The voice of your intuition will bring a sense of calm, clarity, truth, and relief. It can be counterlogical, so it may not make complete sense in the moment, but the less you reason with or resist it, the easier it will be to tune in to the guidance.

Subconscious Mind

Your subconscious mind is a rich and substantial source of intuitive wisdom. It's a vast resource that stores your daily behaviors, habits, and moods. It's where your short-term memories live—the ones that are easily accessible by the conscious mind at any time, such as your address, your birth date, and what you ate for dinner last night.

Your subconscious mind is always switched on and aware of your surroundings (even while you sleep) through your five physical senses. It filters a boundless amount of incoming information from your senses and sends only the important information to the conscious mind—because you simply cannot be conscious of everything in your environment. The subconscious is in control when you do things without conscious thinking—like driving a familiar route or making a cup of tea—because of an accumulation of past experiences that makes it easier to do things without full, conscious attention. This is part of intuitive living; we all have these habits.

Your subconscious mind is strongly connected to the conscious and unconscious minds, *and* it works independently. It obeys conscious thoughts, so the more you hold positive or negative thoughts, the more they will be real, all the way down to your unconscious mind. The subconscious mind communicates what is needed to the conscious mind through emotions, sensations, images, and dreams, but it doesn't use words. This is why your intuition doesn't use words when it's guiding you.

What comes into your life will either *feel* aligned with your true nature or it won't. There's no discussion or dissertation required. When there's a conversation *about the feeling*, you know you're reasoning with your intuitive guidance from your conscious mind. There's no harm in thinking through a decision so long as you clearly trust and honor what you receive from your intuitive, wholehearted self.

Physical Senses

Your five physical senses of touch, hearing, sight, smell, and taste are constantly giving you impressions, information, and feedback. They are always in the present moment and only ever tuned in to what is real. As they consistently help you navigate your way through life, your brain may misinterpret what your senses detect (like when a stick poking into your ankle feels like a snake), but the raw information from your senses is always accurate.

Many teachers, guides, and writers downplay the physical senses in favor of the inner psychic senses when it comes to living intuitively, but from my experience and research, the physical senses feed your intuition, while the inner senses supply information to insight (more on this soon).

All the information you receive from your five senses goes straight into your subconscious mind; from there, there isn't much that makes it into the conscious mind. You only ever have one or two senses in focus while you're engaged in a task; the others fade when not consciously required. Most of the time, you simply take your senses for granted, so you're most likely to be consciously aware of your senses when something in your environment stands out from the rest—like a spider on a wall, burning toast, a rock in your shoe, or the moment when you bite into something unexpectedly hot—or when you actively tune in to your senses.

Your intuitive understanding of life is developed through experience. If your experience tells you what your bedroom looks like, then intuitively you'll know when something is different and perhaps putting you in danger, like a spider on a wall. Intuitively, you know there's something different. Instinctively, you're prepared to do something about it … quickly.

It's the same reason why you're so physically alert with your senses when you're walking through a country you've never been in before. Everything is so new and interesting. When you're at home or in a familiar place, you don't take time to tune in to your senses as much. This sense of familiarity plays an important role in living intuitively. If you've held the same job for many years, your intuition will grow stronger with experience. And if you take time to listen to and honor it, you'll make wholehearted, creative, and beneficial decisions faster at work without relying on your logical mind all the time.

Your incredible senses aren't just your practical connection to your world; they're also your access to living pleasurably. Consciously diving into your senses to explore life is one of the most beautiful ways of feeling truly alive and awake. It doesn't mean overwhelming your being by striving to be in tune with everything all at once, it means slowing down to a more pleasurable pace so that you're able to mindfully experience your world as you wish rather than by accident.

Sensory walks are a healing and gently stimulating way of connecting to your senses. Intuitively strolling through nature while using all five of your senses to explore the luscious environment around you will help you tune in to your senses in everyday moments. This is one way of creating space for your intuition to come alive.

Your senses heighten your awareness of the world around you. When you consciously tune in to your senses, you will notice what pleases you. As you come to embrace what feels good to your whole self, I encourage you to ask yourself, "What is it that pleases me the most in this moment?" What pleases you is not to be ignored, dismissed, or belittled; it is your truth, and all that your intuition is asking you to do is to honor your truth. Learn to decipher the pleasures of your ego (false or fear-based pining) from the pleasures of your Soul (healthy, sacred yearnings). Your ego comes from fear and craves stifling stability, while your Soul speaks of love and welcomes conscious change. Your ego is not interested in your highest good; your Soul only cares for what serves your

Highest Self. Your ego is obsessed with physical pleasure; your Soul delights in it without attachment.

Sensual pleasures bring the experience of being human to life. Think of the last juicy peach you ate, the last sunset you witnessed, the last hug from a close friend, the last time you lit your favorite candle, or the last time you heard a treasured song. Your whole being was lifted higher, your vibration rose, and you may have experienced bliss, healing, or contentment. Pleasure feels good, relaxes the body, and opens us up to a deeper intuitive connection.

Your intuition wants you to be content and truly happy. It may also save your life when it works powerfully with your instinct. Let me illustrate this with a fascinating story from a professor who led a study on intuition. He tells the example of a Formula One driver who stopped suddenly during a race as he approached a hairpin bend. What he couldn't see was a pileup of cars on the other side of the bend; and yet, he stopped in time.

After the race when he was asked why he stopped, he simply said it was an intuitive feeling that he acknowledged. Curious researchers spent time with him, playing the race from different angles until he was able to identify what information had fed his intuitive nudge. As the professor explained, "In hindsight (the driver) realized that the crowd, which would have normally been cheering him on, wasn't looking at him coming up to the bend but was looking the other way in a static, frozen way. That was the cue. He didn't consciously process this, but he knew something was wrong and stopped in time."[3] It turns out it was his intuitive connection to his subconscious mind—through his five senses— that alerted him to an apparent danger around the bend, and the

3. Hodgkinson, Langan-Fox, and Sadler-Smith, "Intuition: A fundamental bridging construct in the behavioural sciences," 1–27.

instinctive response from his body—foot to the brake—saved him. There are so many other ways in which our senses guide us and enrich our lives. In chapter six, I'll discuss this further.

When you're tuned in to your physical sense of self, you're in a state of *presence* rather than a state of *analysis*. Instead of rationalizing, reasoning with, or judging the moment, you're simply being with it and experiencing life. That's when intuition flourishes beyond what you can imagine with your mind, because the rational mind, although a great companion, is how you live logically, not intuitively.

Heart Center

Your heart is the strongest physical organ and the energetic center of your intuitive being. Physically, it expands with every beat it makes (as does the ribcage with every breath); energetically, it has the most far-reaching EMF of any part of your body; and emotionally, it's an expansive place of love where all emotions feel safe.

Your amazing heart, the first organ created in utero, actually sends more information to the brain than the brain sends to the heart. Research at the HeartMath Institute (a nonprofit organization that helps people find alignment with their intuition) has shown that "the heart communicates to the brain in four major ways: neurologically (through the transmission of nerve impulses), biochemically (via hormones and neurotransmitters), biophysically (through pressure waves), and energetically (via electromagnetic field interactions)."[4] Your heart uses all of these richly intertwined systems to tell your brain what is needed and to listen to the brain's response.

4. McCraty, *Science of the Heart*, 3.

Your heart is the physical part of you that is most deeply connected to your Soul. Although your Soul isn't limited to one area of your body, you can access it intentionally through your heartspace in the center of your chest, the middle of the whole. Your heart has an intimate attachment to the Soul, making it your all-knowing, all-seeing visceral guide that can lead you along the path that your Soul has planned for you. Being unlimited in knowledge and power, your heart energy knows your past, present, and future, a knowing that has been seen through the eyes of science.[5]

The heart's energy field is eternally wise. As I touched on previously, the brain, heart, and stomach all have their own EMFs around them. So does every other organ, but these three are the most significant. Up until recently, experts assumed that the brain had the strongest, but research from the HeartMath Institute has shown that the electric *and* magnetic energy waves coming from the heart are substantially more powerful than those from the brain. In fact, the heart's electrical field is up to one hundred times stronger than the brain's, while the heart's magnetic field is around five thousand times stronger than the brain's.[6]

The pulsating, spirited, and robust EMF of your heart is continuously making waves in your mind, body, and surroundings. Your heart's energy is also affected by other living beings, the energy of the earth, and electronic devices.

Always remember, your habits have a deep impact on your heart. The way you breathe, the emotions you hold on to or release, the thoughts you select—these are all critical to how fluidly the energy of your heart flows and how fluently it communicates.

---

5. McCraty, Atkinson, and Bradley, "Electrophysiological Evidence of Intuition," 133–143.

6. McCraty, *The Energetic Heart*, 1.

The heart is physically, energetically, and spiritually your strongest guiding force. When your heart is in charge and you are in flow, the ingenious intuitive influx never ceases to create miracles and magic, abundance and alignment, contentment and connection.

Energetic Spirit

Your spirit is your palpable energy, the unseen lifeforce of your magnificent being. The amazing thing about energy, as Einstein famously noted, is that it cannot be created or destroyed; it can only be changed from one form to another. You can't build or burn it, only transmute or transform it.

Each of your thoughts, feelings, emotions, actions, and words holds a particular energetic vibration. So does the food you eat, the objects in your house, the clothes you wear, the phone you use, the paper you write on, the people you meet, everything in nature, every room you walk into, every home, every building, every town, and every country.

When you meet someone else, you're sensing their energy and they're tuning in to yours, whether you're both conscious of it or not. If you trust and honor what you feel, you will know on a subconscious level—before your rational thought kicks in—if they are an energetic match for you. This is the energetic dance that takes place when people meet. Some days you have a deep impact on others, and some days they influence you. Some people you meet feel like an easy, compatible, energetic fit; other people feel abrasive or at odds with your energy.

Think of an emotion you'd like to hold in your heart. It could be self-acceptance, delight, unconditional love, freedom, amusement, bliss, satisfaction, or devotion. Feel it deeply. Hold it there for as long you need to. No one can take it away from you. If a lower emotion comes along to cloud over it, simply witness and feel it, then let it go. The more you tune in to your own energy and create what you wish to experience, the more you will be able to tune in to the energy of other people, objects, ideas, and situations that you wish to understand on an intuitive level. This is how you color your life and navigate the world intuitively.

· Practice ·
Heart–Led Intuition Soul Prompts

Let's take a loving look at the greatest force within your being: your intuition. Sit with these questions with an open mind and a willing heart. Feel into the answers in meditation or your notebook without the need to be right or perfect.

If your heart doesn't use words, how does intuition feel to you? What does expansion feel like in your body? How does your energetic being light up at the thought of something that's aligned with your deepest truth?

How has your intuition led you lovingly toward your Soul's purpose? Have you ever followed an unexpected nudge toward a person or job that turned out to be wholeheartedly life-changing? Have you ever left a job simply because it didn't feel right? Do you share acts of kindness in your community according to your inner guidance and intuitive understanding of your community's needs?

How conscious are you of your physical senses? How does it feel to tune in to them and live life pleasurably through them? What can you do today to feel into your world more? Can you play music that elevates your energy? Can you eat mindfully? Can you look at nature in wordless wonder? Can you create with your hands? Are there natural fragrances you could surround yourself with?

What emotions are you able to intentionally generate to raise your vibration? Take a deep breath and invite the emotion in, then let all blocks to it be released with the out breath.

Spend time this week noticing the energetic field around your heart and come back to your journal to write about how it feels, how it dances with other energetic fields, and how it wants to be nourished and heard.

Guide 3: Insight

Insight is the most recent development in human evolution as far as self-awareness goes. It's essentially when you receive new information that merges with what you already know to provide a new understanding or a fresh perspective.

Recognizing Insight

Insights are conscious recognition and cosmic creativity. They're stimulating ideas and information that come from the earthly plane, perhaps while reading a book, having a conversation, watching a video, or otherwise connecting with new knowledge. They also come out of "nowhere," often while walking through nature, meditating, drifting off to sleep, taking a shower, enjoying a massage, praying—anytime you're relaxed and open-minded. Insights that pop into your mind out of the blue may come from various sources, including Spirit (Great Spirit, Spirit Guides, Loved Ones, or Archangels). The deeper you're connected to Spirit, the more insights you'll receive from the higher dimensions. However, insights don't only come through to psychics or seers; anyone can receive insights from an endless range of sources.

As you read this book, you'll experience the gift of insight. When a fresh idea resonates with your own truth, you'll uncover a new layer of self-awareness in a way that stirs you from your reading leisure and awakens the wisdom within.

Insights are related to the neocortex part of the brain, the most modern part to evolve. The two large cerebral hemispheres that make up this part of the brain are responsible for the development of human language, abstract thought, imagination, and consciousness. The neocortex is two to three million years old—quite young compared to the limbic system (one hundred fifty million years old) and reptilian brain (five hundred million years old).

Logic, reason, and language are enormously important, but when you rely on guidance from your logical mind *over* your intuitive heart, you place emphasis on a life of expectations and regulations, limits and judgments, rights and wrongs, and exact reasoning. You leave no space for creativity, emotions, feelings, and flow. In order to fulfill your highest potential, you need to live from the empowered combination of your wise brain and your wild heart within the grounded roots of your belly.

Conscious Mind

Your conscious mind is where insights land. In spiritual terms, *conscious* means aware of self and others and awake to a higher truth, a divinity that transcends the physical realm. Living consciously means living in a way that honors the self and others and acknowledges the role and presence of Spirit in all beings.

Being physically unconscious means being in a comatose state. Being spiritually unconscious means living without any real awareness of yourself or how you relate to others and anything outside of the physical realm. If you're not tuned in to the universe outside of the material plane, it's difficult to receive information from Spirit. Insights—spiritual or earthly—readily drop into the minds of the conscious and curious ones who listen to others with an open mind, even if they don't agree with everything they hear.

Psychologically, your conscious mind consists of all that you are aware of in this present moment. It's the conscious mind that directs your attention and awareness and communicates to your outer and inner worlds through speech, pictures, writing, movement, and thought. Your conscious mind is open to insights and can imagine anything new and unique. It's unlimited; it's the eternal spring from which your *aha* moments flow.

As you dwell in conscious presence without your ego stealing your peace, you can intentionally open to receive insights.

Brain Connection

Your brain is where insights are received and organized. Your brain, specifically the neocortex, is your focus mechanism; it's the savvy instrument that discovers new possibilities and information and either acts on them or files them away for later. Your brain is an incredible, inimitable, influential processor. However, it's not meant to lead you, only to inspire you and stimulate the body. When the heart leads, the brain's powers flourish because it thinks and causes action in alignment with love and potential.

Neuroscientists have noted that insights can be cultivated when people are in a happy and relaxed mood.[7] As you may imagine, it's difficult to force your mind to discover insights under pressure. There must be an act of letting go, relaxing your overthinking mind, and calming your body's systems to create space for insights. Create moments of quiet in your day—make time to daydream, reflect, journal, and be at peace to open your life to more regular inspiration. As you do this, you will awaken to a more exciting, adventur-

---

7. Kounios and Beeman, "The *Aha!* Moment," 210–216.

ous, and spirited way of living. Your brain is so eternally capable, so endlessly imaginative, that when it is put to good use, it raises the bar, and life becomes fertile and an inspiration to others, too.

Spiritual Energy

Your spiritual energy is the bridge between insight and you. If you're spiritual, if you believe in a divinity of sorts, then you're likely open to insights dropping into your mind from the universe as divine guidance. Insights from Spirit could come from any of your Spirit Guides, Archangels, Loved Ones, or directly from the voice of your Soul. The more you trust in Spirit, the more you'll find that insights land in your lap just as you need them—without an obvious source.

While intuitive information comes through outer physical senses, insights come from inner psychic senses. You may receive visions (clairvoyance), hear messages (clairaudience), feel things (clairsentience), or simply know information (claircognizance). As a psychic myself, I mostly see and hear information, but I'm open to receiving insights however they are meant to come to me. These inner senses become more perceptive and accurate as you allow and trust in them and grow spiritually.

Inner Senses

Clairvoyance, meaning clear vision, is when you visually perceive messages from Spirit with your third eye. It's similar to daydreaming visually with your eyes open or closed. Clairvoyants use their inner sight to see mental images—which may be literal or symbolic, subtle or clear.

Clairaudience, meaning clear audio, is when you are conscious of sounds, words, music, or other noise coming into your inner ear from Spirit. Occasionally it will come through the outer ear, but it's almost always heard within. Clairaudience is the gift that most—but not all—channelers use as they bring through messages from Spirit.

Claircognizance, meaning clear knowing, is the ability to know things directly through Spirit that you could have no other way of knowing.

Clairsentience, meaning clear sensation, is when you receive information from a feeling within the whole body or particular areas of the body that goes beyond physical feelings and cannot be explained logically.

Clairempathy, meaning clear emotions, is the gift of an empath, a person who is highly sensitive to the emotions of people, animals, and places. It's used to sense the emotion or physical condition of another.

Other lesser-known gifts that are just as powerful are *clairscent*, meaning clear smelling; *clairtangency*, or psychometry, meaning clear touching; and *clairgustance*, meaning clear tasting.

I regularly have deeply spiritual and practical insights come to me during a reading, healing, or mentoring session with a client. Almost all my daily meditations come with an insight from a guide in Spirit, from nature, or simply from my Highest Self. Sometimes they even appear out of thin air, like a thought or a whisper from beyond. I can also go after insights myself as I don't believe they're only spontaneous accidents ready to land in the lap of the fortunate. I often dive into a meditation with a question and readily expect that Spirit will deliver an answer that feels complete (as long as I trust divine timing and let go of expectations). This is how you open your third eye and psychic abilities, by asking, diving, seeing, hearing, trusting, and acknowledging with gratitude.

I've had brilliant insights in the bath and shower (and you bet I didn't have a notepad nearby to write them down), while driving, in the middle of a delicious date with my husband, and just before falling asleep. When my energy is relaxed and happy, I'm open to receiving all I need and desire in a way that is best for me. The same is happening to you right now as you read this book; each page is an opening for you to access insights.

· PRACTICE ·
Mind's Insight Soul Prompts

I believe in the unlimited power of the mind. By getting to know the process of receiving insights, my world has opened up to new potentials and fortuitous happenings. I want to encourage you to let go of any thought that feels limiting or any story that paints you as unworthy of earthly or spiritual insights. You are a miracle. Anything is possible. Take some time now to journal or meditate your way through these questions.

When was the last time you experienced a profound insight? What were you doing and how were you feeling? When did you last watch a documentary and what did you learn? Have you had an interesting conversation lately that has opened your mind to new possibilities? What is the most exciting insight you've learned so far from this book that has changed the way you see or experience your world?

What inner senses do you believe are your strongest? How do you experience a guided meditation—visually, audibly, emotionally, or another way? Do you consciously use your inner senses to understand your world or receive guidance from Spirit?

Have you experienced insights from Spirit? Was it a surprise or did you ask to receive? Who do you connect with—or who would you like to connect with—to receive spiritual insight, and for what purpose? Are you open to receiving insights as a natural part of conscious living?

What does the term *Great Spirit* (or *God*) mean to you? How does Great Spirit show up in your life? How open are you to the voice of your Soul? If you're not familiar with the voice of your Soul, take a moment to open to it, the real you, and experience the vast light and love within. Take your time with this; try it every day for a week and see how it unfolds.

Chapter 3
ALIGNMENT WITH YOUR SOUL

"When we align with our wholeness we rise from the inside out, and then we are able to share the highest manifestation of ourselves with the world."
—VICTORIA L. WHITE

You are a reflection of the universe in a uniquely brilliant and cosmically vibrant way. Universes tend to flow according to their flawless, inherent rhythm. As you connect to and become intimate with your instinct, intuition, and insight, you will notice when you are in or out of alignment. Alignment is simply harmony and communion between mind, body, and spirit; instinct, intuition, and insight; gut, heart, and brain. It's when everything within you leans toward the truth of your Soul. Alignment is when your entire being is living in balance and flow. If you've never experienced alignment before, this might happen for a moment here and there to begin with, but with practice, you can join these moments together so that alignment is the full experience of your life. Self-awareness helps with this process, as does positivity, trust, and a devotion to honesty. By the end of this book, you will have learned many ways of opening to your self-awareness and living in alignment.

One of the ways you can thoroughly understand your inner universe and what needs more care for deeper alignment is by looking at your chakras.

Get to Know Your Chakras

When you get to know your chakras, you can see where your inner guides fit into your energetic form in such a detailed and accessible way. You can easily work with your chakras yourself; any way that you heal and balance them will affect your instinct, intuition, and insight in effective and often surprising ways. (See chapter nine for specific ways to balance your chakras.)

Chakras look and act like spinning wheels, so it's no surprise that *chakra* is Sanskrit for "wheel." When your chakras spin effortlessly, they create a healthy and harmonious flow of energy up and down your spine called *kundalini energy*.

I've learned about chakras from many books, many healers and clients, and many meditations over the years. I love how they communicate directly with me through color or visions about the health of my, or a client's, body. You will experience them in your own unique way according to your inner psychic senses.

Chakras are the anchor points of your entire energy field. There are seven main chakras within the body, with more inside, above, and below your physical form. Each chakra relates to different colors (due to the speed at which they spin), elements, physical/mental/emotional areas, senses, and developmental cycles in your life.

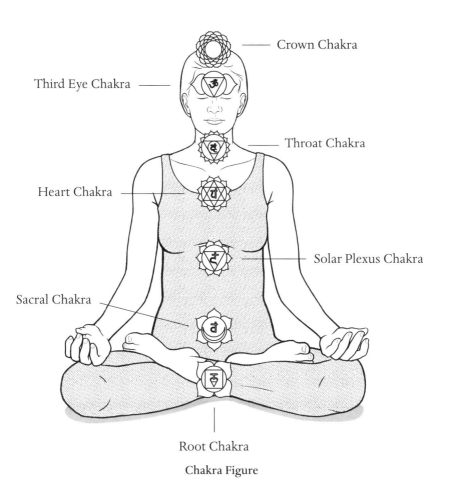

Chakra Figure

Unbalanced, blocked, small, overactive, or underactive chakras can lead to unfavorable changes to your mental, emotional, physical, and spiritual health. When you connect with each chakra and learn to feel into them, you are able to awaken and heal each of them. Healing your chakras is an empowering way to heal your past, your thoughts, your energy, and your body, and bring you a greater level of thriving health and wellness.

Chakras that are balanced, clear, and vibrant are able to guide your energy—and your life—seamlessly and powerfully. When you heal the lower chakras, you calm the fear of your *instinct*, allowing it to keep you safe and on purpose with strong roots. When you open the heart chakra of your *intuition*—and neighboring chakras—allowing love to flow in and out, you regain a steady stream of energetic connection and are able to welcome intuitive guidance. And when you clear the way for your upper chakras to draw inspiration and light (intelligence) from Source energy, you open up to vivid *insight*.

Let's move through each chakra from the root to the crown.

Root Chakra

Color: Red

Related to: Safety, survival, family, tribe, physical nourishment

Element: Earth

Sense: Smell

Affirmation: I am safe, healthy, and grounded. I am successful and abundant.

Healing prompts: How safe did you feel as a child? How secure do you feel day to day? How often do you ground yourself in nature? Do you feel naturally successful? Are you open to abundance in all forms?

The base "root" chakra carries with it the instinctive guidance from your ancestors, the tribes of your familial bloodlines, and the human race as a whole. It's where your instinct originates, and it's related to the adrenals that activate your fight-or-flight response to keep you safe. When you heal the aspects connected to your root chakra, you're grounding your instinct, which will help you feel less flighty or easily scared.

Sacral Chakra

Color: Orange

Related to: Emotions/feelings, creativity, sexuality, ethics, control

Element: Water

Sense: Taste

Affirmation: I enjoy life's pleasures without guilt. I am creative, sensual, and adaptable. I allow emotions to flow through me in a way that feels free.

Healing prompts: What does sexual energy feel like to you? What emotions are you uncomfortable expressing? What emotions from others make you feel uncomfortable? What does it feel like to be in creative flow? What pleasures do you enjoy wholeheartedly?

As you awaken the second "sacral" chakra, your instinct develops further, you find your creativity takes on new forms, your emotions don't control you, and your pleasure does not invite guilt or shame.

Solar Plexus Chakra

Color: Yellow

Related to: Intellect, confidence, personal power, structure, will, trust

Element: Fire

Sense: Sight

Affirmation: I am aware of my wants, needs, and desires. I am confident and empowered. I relish my wisdom and sense of humor.

Healing prompts: Do you get what you want with honesty and gratitude, force and coercion, or victimhood and attachments? Are you judging or accepting of yourself? Do you value your intellect as unique and worthy?

Your third "solar plexus" chakra is the center of your personal power, self-esteem, and self-respect and is directly connected to the gut. It's related to your personal sense of safety and security, inner power, and self-esteem. Once this chakra has developed, your instinct is fully connected and awake, and when the first three chakras are clear and balanced, your instinct is able to keep you safe, grounded, and connected with ease and love.

Heart Chakra

Color: Green

Related to: Love, compassion, healing, relationships, intuition, anger

Element: Air

Sense: Touch

Affirmation: I am compassionate, loving, and lovable. I allow my intuition to guide me with faith and grace. I value and honor my relationships with self and others.

Healing prompts: Do you feel worthy of unconditional love from yourself and others? Are you compassionate toward those around you who are different, difficult, or suffering? Does your heart feel open and light? Are you guided by your wholehearted and wise intuition? Have you tapped into the healer within?

The fourth "heart" chakra is related to intuition, love, compassion, and healing. It infuses its energy into how you relate to others, to love, and to the energy around you. Unconditional self-love is the core of a flowing heart chakra; this is an important step in nourishing your intuition. This chakra is the meeting place of the upper insight chakras and lower instinctive chakras. This is why I use words like "heart-centered" and "wholehearted," because when we are completely balanced, we are living aligned and centered within the heart of our being.

Throat Chakra

Color: Blue

Related to: Truth, expression, guidance, communication

Element: Sound

Sense: Hearing

Affirmation: I freely express my truth. I am comfortable sharing my unique voice with others. I listen to my inner voice when it guides me with love.

Healing prompts: Are there any gifts that you are stifling? Are you at ease communicating honestly with others? Are you open to listening empathetically? How did you trust yourself today?

Your intuitive voice is related to your fifth "throat" chakra, as this is the seat of communication and guidance. This voice comes straight from and into the heart, so it makes sense that the more love you pour into and out of your life, the clearer your intuition and voice of truth can be received, heard, and articulated.

Third Eye Chakra

Color: Indigo

Related to: Insight, truth, inner wisdom, psychic abilities, inner vision

Element: Light

Sense: Knowing

Affirmation: I am insightful, wise, and tuned in to my natural psychic potential.

Healing prompts: Are you easily able to surrender old beliefs when new truths present themselves? Do you pay attention to the higher realms and what they have to offer? Are you in touch with what you believe and also open to hear what others believe without becoming defensive or preachy? Do you trust the unexpected epiphanies that you experience?

The sixth "third eye" chakra relates to insight and wisdom. Most teachings over the ages state that intuition is related to the third eye, and although they're undoubtedly strongly related, I see this chakra as the center of insight: clear thinking and wisdom from your Highest Self and Spirit. It's where you receive wisdom from the Divine and your Soul (one and the same)—truth that potentially rearranges and realigns your beliefs, perceptions, values, and the meaning that weaves its thread through the essence of your life.

Crown Chakra

Color: White / purple
Related to: Connection to Source, spirituality, purpose
Element: Consciousness
Sense: None
Affirmation: I believe in miracles. I lean toward bliss. I am wise and aware. I am one with Source energy.
Healing prompts: Do you feel connected to all life—the earth, plants, animals, and people—or detached and separate? How do you see the bigger, divine picture, and how does that enlighten or impact your path? How do you direct your curiosities and thirst for greater knowledge?

Your seventh "crown" chakra is your connection to Source. When this is clear and strong, you are in touch with your purpose and the oneness of life. When you actively nourish this chakra, your consciousness expands, and you are able to access insight from Spirit. It's the place from which you can access the vastness and guidance of the higher realms.

LET ALIGNMENT FLOW

It helps if you don't *identify* with your inner guides or chakras, but rather sit in the conscious seat of your Soul as a witness to all that you are. When you genuinely feel this on a deep level—that you are not your physical, emotional, or mental selves—you will feel true freedom beyond words. Take a step back from your thoughts and emotions and simply watch them play out. Let them melt away and fall in love with life without the usual mental commentary, or "thought baggage" as Eckhart Tolle calls it. Revel in the sweet serendipity of living consciously.

When you're in peaceful alignment with all that you are, when you're living according to what you know to be true for you, then you're connected to the most important wisdom and grace of all … yours.

· RITUAL ·
Alignment Meditation

This is one of the most powerful meditations I've ever shared with clients and workshop groups. When you get to know it well, you'll be able to move through it on your own with your eyes closed whenever you're feeling out of alignment or simply desiring to tune in to the free flow of wisdom within.

Sit comfortably in your chair, feet flat on the floor, hands resting gently in your lap, back straight. Breathe deeply through your nose into your belly, let the breath flow effortlessly out, and let all thoughts fade away. Focus gently on your breathing, your body, and the spirit that resides within. Take a few more deep belly breaths in your own time to relax and let your thoughts fade into the background.

Let your face, jaw, and shoulders relax. Feel the weight of your arms and legs. Keep breathing deeper, deeper, deeper. Feel the earth beneath you, supporting you. Let go and surrender to the earth. Let it hold you.

Now take a moment to open your inner senses to the golden light that lives in your heart center. A light so pure and warm. A light that is your own luminous Soul, your still and quiet presence, always there, always guiding, always loving. Feel the deep grace of this light as it moves down your body, through the gut with a healing force, and into the earth. Imagine it moving through the layers of Mother Earth all the way down to the core, to the heart of our precious planet. Feel what that feels like to connect your power with nature … and then slowly draw up the earth's energy through the layers, up through your feet, and into the center of your being.

Now see this grounded and activated light move up through the top of your head, your crown, all the way into the sky, higher and higher until it reaches Source energy. Feel the connection with Great Spirit, the power and unlimited light and unconditional love in the highest dimension. Bring this energy slowly down into the crown of your head, down to the center of your being. Allow this light to expand and slowly surround you in a golden ball.

Savor this feeling. Hold it for a moment, appreciating the healing and illumination of your three inner guides as well as Mother Earth and Source. See this energy all around your body. Feel the warmth cocooning you. Bask in the light. Give thanks for all that you are connected to. Stay with this healing sensation as long as you need to. Know that luminous alignment is always available to you anytime you need it.

When you're ready, wriggle your toes and feet. Move your fingers; stretch your hands and arms. Rock your head gently from side to side and slowly open your eyes. How do you feel? This sensation is an inner anchor for you as you move forward along your spiritual journey. You can come back to this meditation, this feeling, this light, as often as you need to. This is home. This is sacred connection. This is alignment.

Part Two
SIX STEPS FOR THRIVING INTUITIVELY

Growing and strengthening your self-awareness and living from your inner intelligence is essential to living with purpose, ease, joy, and abundance. The first section of this book gave you a deep and wide understanding of your intuition, insight, and instinct, creating a palpable grounding for your path.

In part two, I'll be explaining six ways to fortify the bond to your inner self with practical, hands-on, playful, and soulful ideas, exercises, rituals, and inspiration. There are also plenty of stories to show you how this process has unfolded in my life and in the lives of others.

This is a fluid map, not a strict six-step methodology, so I encourage you to embrace this approach in whatever way you desire. Play with the suggestions and don't get too attached to what I do or how I do it. Just follow what feels best for you and your wise heart.

Here are the essentials of the six steps:

Breathe: Connecting within begins with conscious and calm breathing to bring you into the present, precious moment.

Surrender: Letting go of whatever is unwanted, toxic, or negative in your life will create nourishment for your intuition to powerfully bloom, safety for your instinct to be grounded, and space for your insight to receive enlightenment.

Connect: Developing uninhibited ways to lovingly connect to all parts of you—as well as to Spirit—opens the inner and outer channels to receive wisdom, love, and healing.

Trust: Having real confidence and faith in your truth will strengthen your connection and allow it to expand infinitely.

Honor: Following through and actioning what your inner wisdom has asked of you is crucial. Knowing without doing creates a block to intuitive progress.

Nourish: Taking care of your whole being with love, gentleness, and respect is essential for your mind, body, and energy to grow in alignment with your Highest Self.

Each step is valuable as you open to new ways of living from your heart.

With a little practice, the processes that I describe in detail in the chapters that follow will become effortless rituals that you can come to at any time. Remember, you are immensely intuitive already. With each of these steps, you're shining brighter with the luminous energy of your true self.

Chapter 4
BREATHE

"Let your heart breathe, sweet soul.
Breathe until you remember life's beauty again.
Breathe as much as you need to,
until you remember your own beauty again.
Take as much time as you need. The world will wait."

—S. C. LAURIE

A conscious breath is one of the purest experiences of self-awareness because it instantly brings a gentle awareness to your body and allows your precious lifeforce to flow untethered. Your breath is the spirited, life-giving pulse and rhythm of your being; breathing is an act that is automated and yet completely and blissfully under your control.

In this first important step, I'll guide you through ideas, stories, and practices to help you anchor into the sweet nothingness of your sacred breath.

STIFLING RELIGION
TO BREATHTAKING SPIRITUALITY

I spent the first half of my life tucked inside a swaddle of religion. It was restrictive and uncompromising and made it kind of hard for me to breathe.

Religion taught me a lot from a young age. It gave me an easy relationship with Great Spirit, access to Jesus and Mother Mary, the tools to pray, a community who cared about me on a Soul level, scores of friends, and a love of storytelling. Going to church was great for my spirit in so many ways. But after twenty years of hearing the same messages, it all began to feel unnecessarily fearful and profoundly condescending. Eventually, I became sure of a few things: I wasn't a "sinner," I didn't need to be "saved," there is no fiery hell in the afterlife, and we're not judged for everything we do "wrong."

I needed to leave. *I needed to breathe.* So, I flew free.

I gave up the hold that religion had on my life and created space to hear myself, see with open eyes, and live from a curious heart. I began the search for what could bring meaning and divinity into my heart without the limiting, patriarchal strings attached.

There I was, twenty years old, confused, wide-eyed, completely naïve, and craving something I couldn't even name. I'd love to say that I reached out for help and slowly, gracefully, found my way onto a richly creative and inspiring spiritual path, but instead I waded through the murky waters of alcohol, drugs, smoking, casual sex, and other flavors of desperation and self-disrespect. I was trying to *feel good* to numb my past and liberate my heart. But I had a palate for irreverent adventure, so I rebelled consistently against my better judgment.

Some days I could hear the call of my heart singing like a forgotten bird in the night, but I was working hard—too hard for my sensitive nature. I was drinking way more than my body could handle. I was dabbling in drugs. And I was confusing sex for acceptance and love. With all that going on, there was no space left to listen.

Eventually, and after much heartache, I slowed down. I began to tune inward, just a touch. I felt the flickering flames of self-love. I met the man who'd be my husband and found sex with only one person to be the most liberating sexual act of all. I realized drugs were far too much trouble for a sensitive Soul like me. I calmed down around alcohol (though it would take me a long time to be free from it). I left the eighty-five-hour-a-week job ... and I found yoga.

Every time I rolled out my yoga mat, I unfurled a little more of my crumpled Soul. Every time I struck a warrior pose, I unleashed the goddess within. Every time I breathed with the postures, I found my true power. One morning, a friend invited me to her yoga class. It was heart-opening and rather blissful. Afterward, we went back to her place for a cup of tea.

She pulled out a deck of tarot cards for us to play with, which triggered a defensive religious response that gratefully and quickly subsided. As I shuffled her well-worn cards, my heart whispered, *Show me what it means to live spiritually, soulfully, with the presence of Great Spirit but without religion, with heaven but not hell; show me a way.* Soon enough, a handful of cards were laid before me by my intuitive friend. The Celtic Cross. My eyes mesmerized, my Soul stirring, each card was flipped over, each message loud and clear, each answer absorbed into my whole being with previously unknown delight.

I can't remember all the cards from that day, but for as long as I live, I'll never forget the very last card: the Hermit. Standing alone at the end of a cliff, the Hermit scared me. He looked old, sad, and alone. I thought this meant I'd live a long and lonely life, but my friend calmed me with her insight. She said I'd go solo on my spiritual adventure—that I'd find the answers within.

That reading changed everything, though I couldn't imagine how profoundly at the time. It was the day my spiritual journey really began. Ever since then, I've carved my own path: stubbornly, joyfully, imprecisely, organically, selfishly, wildly, courageously. And finally, as I live according to my truth, I can breathe easy.

THE JOY OF SLOW, MINDFUL BREATHING

My prayer is that all beings live free and breathe easy. If your life doesn't afford you the pleasure and freedom of deep, satisfied breathing, I want to help and encourage you to regularly fill your precious being with full, conscious breaths—the kind that will bring your whole self back to life. From here, the guidance for your life will flow to you much easier. When you breathe, sit gently upright to give your body the best chance at breathing well. Breathe in through your nose until your belly is full—from the pelvic bones up—and then expand your chest with fresh air, too. Now let it all out really slowly through your nose or mouth—whatever feels good. Sigh if you need to. For some, this will be natural and easy; for others, it may take some time to get used to full breathing. Be patient with yourself.

Breathe it all in; let it all out. Slowly, slowly, at your own pace. Keep going until you can feel the gentle power of your lifeforce moving through your whole being. Until you can feel the breath breathing you—your spirit moving your body from within your gut, into your heartspace, and to your brain, stimulating your instinct, intuition, and insight to work freely. Let the breath bring flow into your energetic, emotional, mental, spiritual, and physical systems.

Your breath is the ideal place to start with any intuitive process because it connects you instantly to the energy of your body and draws you out of incessant thinking. Your intuition comes from your physical body and the spirited energy within and around you, not from your logical thoughts. Slow down to breathe, and you will also allow your vagus nerve to facilitate peaceful, healing communication within.

The English word *spirit* comes from the Latin *spiritus*, meaning spirit, Soul, courage, vigor, and *to breathe*. The breath has long been associated with courage and vigor as it summons an inner strength when deep and conscious. It unfurls tension and resistance. It carries you into the present moment where all things are available and possible. Your breath cannot be seen; it connects you to a feeling of nothingness, the most simple and freeing practice of all.

As you keep your deep breathing practice going, let's bring in some visualizations. You might want to imagine what you'd like to breathe in and what you can let go of with the out breath. A few ideas to try …

Breathe in peace, breathe out fear.

Breathe in harmony, breathe out conflict.

Breathe in healing, breathe out tension.

Breathe in joy, breathe out anger.

Breathe in sovereignty, breathe out unworthiness.

Breathe in oneness, breathe out judgment.

Breathe in love, breathe out love.

Breathe in. Breathe out. There is so much joy to be found in a slow, delicious, full breath. When you find comfort and bliss in your breathing, you'll never search outside of yourself for them again.

Deep Breaths: A Portal to Wisdom

Every breath is a collaboration between your rhythmical, cyclical, and intelligent body and the rhythms, cycles, and intelligence of

Mother Earth. *Breathing in* draws air into your lungs, whose job is to absorb the available oxygen so that your body can thrive with fresh energy. *Breathing out* releases carbon dioxide, a biodegradable waste.

If a deep breath is the sweetest route to bliss, then chronic shallow breathing is the swiftest path to stress. Shallow, unconscious breathing is unfortunately the default setting for many; yet it has countless negative, stressful consequences on the mind, body, and Soul. If you continuously breathe this way, your body is always prepared to fight or flight. In this state, you use limited lung capacity, which can cause a build up of toxic carbon dioxide in the blood.

Deep breathing lowers the diaphragm that lives between the lungs and the abdomen to allow the lungs to draw in more air. When you expand the belly, you're not actually bringing air into the gut, you're creating space for the diaphragm to drop down so that the lungs have maximum capacity. This increases the levels of oxygen in the blood and nutrients in the cells as well as produces more endorphins: natural pain-relieving chemicals.

You're more likely to experience greater emotional stability and overall wellness when you breathe deeply because deep breaths also strengthen and stimulate the vagus nerve. When your vagus nerve is strong, it sends a signal to the brain that all is well in your body. When your body is strained, it sends a signal to the brain indicating that you're in a stressful situation, and the brain commands the body accordingly. This means temporarily or indefinitely switching on the sympathetic nervous system, which keeps you safe by dilating pupils, increasing heart rate, shortening breath, and utilizing other functions designed to deal with a real or imagined threat.

The strange thing is, we've reached a point in our evolution as human beings where we spend most of the time with our sympathetic nervous system activated. This means we're *living in* fight-or-flight mode, making us chronically stressed and on edge. Technology, fast-paced lifestyles, disconnection from nature and our bodies, and the never-ending search for perfection are the main contributors to this global anxiety. Debt. Chemicals. Bills. Conflict. Screens. Expectations. News. Social media. Noise. Traffic. Fear. Disease. It all adds up to a relatively rough time on this once-serene planet.

While you're in this state, your instinctual guidance may be uncertain or fearful, while your intuition may not come through so easily. Stress is not a fertile foundation for wholehearted living; it's difficult to hear your heart when your body thinks it's on high alert to stay alive. Although this stress state should be temporary, many people live with stress constantly, compulsively, and unconsciously. If you're focused on being incessantly switched on, pushing your limits, always being available, or carrying a heavy load, you are living in fear. While in this state, it would be nearly impossible to live intuitively.

That's why deep breathing and other calming, grounding exercises are so important to hear the guidance within. They are the portal to the inner wisdom of your entire being.

· RITUAL ·
Box Breathing Exercise

My favorite breathing exercise is so simple and yet extremely effective for those times when I feel stressed. It's called box or square breathing, and it's easy to remember and use wherever you go. All breaths should be in and out of your nose, not your mouth. This allows for slower, calmer breathing and more oxygen to enter your body. Simply count to four as you breathe in, hold your breath for four, breathe out for four, and hold for four again. Don't push yourself to hold your breath if it's uncomfortable; simply play with the speed until you find a rhythm that feels really nourishing, then you can slow it down when you're ready.

CONSCIOUS PAUSES FOR PRESENCE

Take time to mindfully connect with your breath each and every day; it will do more for your intuitive life than you could imagine.

A daily conscious breathing practice creates space for your presence, where your intuitive self can emerge and truly flourish. When you set aside time to get in touch with your beloved breath, you are creating a sacred, conscious pause that will allow the intuitive magic to unfold from inside you, the earthly instinct to hold you strong, and the mystical insight to seep into your being.

With a regular breathing practice, you begin to live in soulful, aligned motion every day. Meditation becomes simpler, deeper. Upsets are less of a big deal. Joy is found in unexpected places. Fluidity and creativity are easily accessed.

Let your deep breaths work their magic in your meditations, body awareness, daydreaming, exercises, communication, decision-making, emotional reactions, and eating. Anytime you find your belly feeling constricted, your chest tight, or your mind overworked … *breathe.*

Any kind of conscious pause that allows you to reflect on your inner world and all that it has to offer is one worth pursuing for the sake of flourishing wellness and self-awareness. If you like routine, choose a time of day that you would like to set aside as your conscious pause. It could be in bed or on the bus, after yoga or before lunch; put it in your phone as a quiet alarm to remind you to pause every day. Try five minutes of deep belly breaths to calm your body, invigorate your mind, and connect to love. Try it with your eyes open or closed while seated, standing, or lying down; go with what works in the moment.

Take notes in your journal after your conscious pause if an insight lands that you want to explore or simply remember.

· PRACTICE ·
Deep Breathing Soul Prompts

As you explore pauses for breathing, you may want to gently and curiously observe your breath without judgment. Any improvement on the quality of your breathing will organically bring you closer to your still and eternal nature from which your centered intuitive guidance can come to you with ease.

How do you normally breathe? With your belly or chest? Fast or slow? Is this creating a calm awareness in your being? If not, how does it make you feel?

How does your body want to be breathed? What feels most nourishing to your body?

How does your body, mind, and Soul feel after a session of soft, deep breathing?

When is the best time of day for you to pause and breathe deeply? As soon as you wake up, just before bed, or as you sit down to eat? How will you remind yourself of this new ritual so that you will honor it each day?

HIGHER AWARENESS AND EARTHY EXPERIENCES

In 2017, I went through an intensely uncomfortable transformation. My body became more acutely sensitive than ever. My psychic abilities were unlocked further. My sleep was a hot mess. My friendships were all shaken up. And the book I'd been writing for years had to be filed away under "maybe not."

It was overwhelming, confusing, and painful. Every time I felt alone or ostracized, every time I couldn't sleep at night, every time I questioned my purpose, my breath would become shallow, and I would fall into a dark cycle of fearful thinking.

Thanks to an understanding of and fondness for meditation and breathing practices, I eventually found my way back to my breath and into my body. Anchored in the breath, I felt reassured in an unspoken way that everything was perfectly fine in a messy yet divinely orchestrated way. It was all an important part of my journey; I just had to surrender to it.

Using my breath as an anchor gave me greater space and perspective in everything that was happening in my life. The breath soothed my body and nudged me toward all I needed to know to bring myself back into alignment, balance, acceptance, surrender, and, ultimately, joy. In the depths of a full breath lay many answers to the mysteries of my suffering.

Breathing helps me understand and appreciate what's really going on. I slow down to my quiet inner rhythm where I can simply and powerfully *be*. I witness without reaction.

As you find your own natural breathing rhythm, your energy will become lighter, brighter, and clearer. This is a sumptuous feeling, so your ego may want to fight it. Don't be scared of living high; you're simply returning to your natural state.

As the breath takes you into a higher vibration along this conscious journey of awakening, you'll need to keep yourself grounded. Grounding is essential, because the more time you spend in the higher realms in communion with your Soul and Spirit, the more you need to feel into the earthiness of your existence—into your body and nature and the physical realm. It's a necessary balance for living on earth as a conscious creature.

There are many ways to do this, but however you can get your bare skin on Mother Earth will suffice. Gardening, beach runs, bushwalks, saltwater baths, eating cooked root vegetables, skinny-dipping, camping, and tree-hugging are all powerfully healing and will bring you back to your body. I also adore beeswax craft, eating with my hands, clay masks, wearing clothing made from natural fibers, and healing with crystals.

Mother Nature holds space like no one else. She grounds your energy. She dissolves your confusion and pain. She wraps her arms around you until you're okay. She shares her wisdom in many profound ways. And she is the reason for our life-giving breath.

If you become too obsessed with breathing and meditation practices, you might feel flighty, ungrounded, and blown about every which way. When this happens, look for ways to ground your being according to your needs and your inner guidance.

Keep in mind that your Soul is always naturally guiding you, so don't overthink it. Your inner wisdom will show you how to live with a healthy balance between higher awareness and earthy connection, between giving and receiving, a simple energetic exchange that your breath mirrors so succinctly. Your heart is the midpoint to higher living and earthy grounding; let it guide you well.

Awakening the Lifeforce of Your Spirit

In the early days of awakening the breath, you may find that something else awakens inside you. Your thoughts may feel raw and honest, sleep habits may change, your body may require different foods, or you may be more psychic, empathic, or receptive. This is your lifeforce stirring, opening you to your Soul on a vibrant new level. You might feel sparkly, bright, and more conscious. You may also feel tentative, uncomfortable, or awkward. It's okay. Growth can be weird. Transformation is rarely comfortable. Conscious living means shedding old, cosy, and fearful ways of thinking and being. Breathe through it. Witness it and accept it for what it is. Do your best not to resist or overthink what is happening. If awkward becomes painful, find a spiritual mentor, join a healing circle, invest in energy healing, or see a professional counselor.

As you connect to your inner wisdom, you will create a greater awareness of self and awaken to your truth. It's impossible not to. This is all part of spiritual awakening. Waking up can happen at any time. For some, it's an overnight wake-up call. For others, it's a slow, organic process, sped up a little by children, partners, illness, grief, career change, or other transitions. Waking up happens for many reasons. Mostly, it's your mind and body aligning to your Highest Self and responding to the pull of your Soul.

Here are some signs of awakening:

- You question *everything*.
- You begin to trust *yourself* first.
- You follow your *heart* over your head.
- Your happiness comes from *within*, not externally.
- You set *boundaries* in place where there once were insecurities.
- You connect to something *bigger* and you recognize oneness.

As I've seen regularly in my own life and in the lives of clients and friends, the biggest block to awakening, expanding, and strengthening your inner connection is fear. Fear of the unknown. Fear of your own greatness. Fear of what other people will think. Fear of releasing attachments to all you have and know.

As simple as it may sound, the best antidote to fear is deep breathing and fueling your thoughts with love. Keep breathing and believing that the unknown is full of abundance and magic. Keep breathing and believing that you are worthy of greatness on all levels. Keep breathing and believing that the right people will be there to support and adore you. Keep breathing and believing that what is aligned with your Soul is worth deep transformation.

Many of us fear failure, a feeling that can paralyze the breath and disconnect us from our wise selves. But there's no such thing as failure when you're on your path. When things go "wrong," it's simply the universe moving you in a different direction. When you feel like you've failed, take a big, compassionate breath, tune in to the truth of what's really happening, and look for the gift in the situation. Don't freeze in fear. Nothing is wrong. Take time to acknowledge that and always come back to love. This process is meant to stir up your foundation so that the seeds you sow will grow into the most abundant, rewarding, satisfying, and loving life possible.

· RITUAL ·
Affirmations for the Breath

If you find meditation difficult, take a moment today to be still while repeating an affirmation. By consciously expressing your gratitude and embracing your breath, you're training your body to flow with the breath while welcoming new beliefs. Slow living may not be possible every day, but a deep breath is always accessible in any moment. Try one or all of these if you like, or create your own with words from your heart.

I am worthy to consciously awaken and live a self-aware life.

I am grateful for my lifeforce and proud to be me.

I fully express myself every day.

I love my body with every breath.

I slow down to the speed of my Soul.

I am safe to travel to the depths of my being.

I accept all of me, however that looks and feels today.
I adore the life I have created.
I am open to receiving guidance with every breath.

AWARENESS AND ACCEPTANCE OF YOUR WHOLE SELF

Belly breathing opens you to a richer awareness of your whole self. When you become aware of all of you and embrace yourself exactly as you are, without labeling or judging, a gentle but radical shift is created in your life.

As you get to know and love yourself deeper, your ego will still be there, hoping to put you back in your place in the seat of fear where it can control you. It might remind you to stay small, to stop thinking you're "so spiritual," or point out what's "wrong" with you that needs "fixing." It will also try to undermine your breathing practice, giving you ten things you could do instead to be more productive.

Notice whatever messages arise from the ego without argument, then go straight back to being blissfully aware. Keep at it. Keep witnessing, accepting, loving, and showing up for your whole self and your wild breath.

The ego makes anything new sound scary because it doesn't like change. I've heard many clients talk about their concerns along their Soul's path, but I can see it's usually the ego talking.

They're scared they won't hear their own inner wisdom clearly … *so they deny it.*

They're scared they won't like what they hear … *so they block the flow.*

They're scared they'll have to do everything they hear … *so they hesitate.*

They're scared that others will think they're selfish ... *so they keep following the crowd.*

Here's the thing: once you've accepted all of yourself (there will be many opportunities throughout this book—and your life—to practice this), you won't have anything left to fear. That sounds radical *because it is.* Knowing yourself is a lifelong journey of discovery, acceptance, and love. It's a journey that allows you to release the fears that are holding you back from living your most abundant life.

Like anything you try, the process will become easier the more you practice. Keep breathing, and no matter what comes to your heart and mind as you breathe, accept it. Accept the anger, jealousy, confusion, frustration, anxiety, bitterness, embarrassment, worry, guilt, shame, despair, disappointment, stress, tension, and anything else you've been taught is "bad," then let it go. This is the beauty of breathing through difficult emotions: the breath becomes the vehicle through which we are able to release heavy emotions and come back to love.

Welcome all this difficulty and negativity, along with all your sweet positivity, with open arms and let it move through you with the breath; let it all dissolve in its own time in the well of love inside. Keep breathing. You're an amazing being.

· PRACTICE ·
Whole Awareness Soul Prompts

As you keep progressing through your journal—or however you enjoy connecting with the prompts in this book—you may be noticing where fear comes in and tries to trip you up and where love comes in to boost your confidence and vibration. Keep noticing both without attachment. Simply be honest. In all things, be loyal to your truth.

How are you being called to anchor into your body today? Does your body need to stretch, eat differently, dance wildly, sing loudly, or have a bath? Feel into your body and allow it to communicate its needs and desires to you.

How do you cultivate peace in your daily life? What brings peaceful thoughts to mind? What makes your body feel immersed in ease? How is your Soul wanting to give you access to deeper contentment?

What powerful emotions have been swirling inside you today? What messages or gifts do they have for you? What thoughts are you attaching to the emotions that aren't necessary or helpful? Can you simply let them be and let them go?

When it comes to self-awareness, is there anything you're scared of? What does your Soul have to say in response? What does love have to offer your fears? Close your eyes and ask the wisdom within what it wants to tell or show you.

· RITUAL ·
A Spirited Prayer

Prayers are visions, requests, yearnings, hopes, dreams, or desires come to life through words. When I pray, I sit in silence and gently focus on my deep breaths until words come from my being and wash through me. With prayers, I tend not to beg for anything, but to instead give thanks for everything while authentically acknowledging my highest desires.

I wrote this prayer for you to witness your awareness and awakening from a sacred point of view. Say this prayer anytime you wish to open to your inner wisdom, your magical presence, with gratitude and eternal worthiness.

As my stillness sacredly awakens the lifeforce of my Soul
May I accept myself and know my truth
May I value my voice, my time, my energy
And may I feel connected to the whole through each breath.

May my sacred heart guide the way
As I lean into each precious moment before me.
Through the willingness to be present
I access a portal to the deepest love.

I am grateful for all that is
For all that I have experienced
And for all that shall be.
So it is.

Chapter 5

SURRENDER

"Surrender is not a weakness; it is a strength.
It takes tremendous strength to
surrender life to the Supreme—to the cosmic unfolding."
—MOOJI

In the moment of surrender, you are free. You've opened your heart, released control, unfurled your grasp on expectations, relinquished judgment, and welcomed a higher, more expansive way of being. Surrender cannot be forced—only allowed. It's the deepest level of grace and will bring miracles into all areas of your life.

If a deep breath is the first step to tune in, surrender naturally follows. In the pages that follow, you'll discover how to surrender and why it's so vital to an intuitive life.

THE ART OF SURRENDER

Surrender is one of the loveliest words to say out loud but can be a real challenge to accomplish. And yet, without surrender, you remain a slave to all you cling to.

Surrendering unhealthy habits, expectations, fears, insecurities, beliefs, ideas, stories, outcomes, attachments, emotions, and worries will feel difficult if you think these are what define you. Perhaps you're afraid that you won't know who you are if you let it all go. You may be unsure if you'll lose yourself in the process or if you'll feel empty and clueless without labels to lean on. But on a Soul level, these attachments are just masks covering the light of your true, spiritual being.

Inside surrender lives a reservoir of peace. The more you surrender, the more peaceful your life becomes. Becoming self-aware is ironically about undoing what you think you know about yourself so that you can sink into your inner spaciousness and slowly reclaim the truth of who you are. The true you will reveal your true path. And in surrendering what is in the way of your truth, you will connect to all you need with deep, sweet clarity.

My close friend Jarka went through a process of deep surrender that she shared with me. Jarka is a hard worker, a fiercely intelligent woman who overflows with motivation and drive. For years, Jarka focused on following the rules that promised her career advancement. Pushing, striving, and forcing were part of her default operating settings. She couldn't see that this yang-driven initiative came from a place of wanting to be praised, approved of, needed, and, often, feared.

Inevitably, Jarka's career came crashing down around her. As it did, she realized that she needed to surrender her identification with her vocation, surrender what she thought success was meant to look like, surrender the corporate games and how they played to her ego, and welcome a life and business guided by her heart. Jarka took to surrender like she previously took to her corporate hustle, and the more time she spent learning about herself, the more confidence she built. The more mindful she became in her life, the more she could distinguish between her ego's voice and that of her intuition.

"The life and business I built as a result of this transformation are nothing short of incredible," she told me. "I feel fulfilled, peaceful, and aligned on most days, and when challenges present themselves, I welcome them, because I know I already have the answers within my inner knowing."

Her transformation took months of curiosity and self-inquiry, of surrendering old habits and reactions that didn't serve her highest interest. This is a valuable process that doesn't happen overnight but requires time and space to open to your truest being. Letting go isn't something that needs to be done all at once; that's an impossible task. Your attachments have been cultivated over many, many years; they are intimately plaited through the fibers of your human self and require endless patience and compassion for the deeply healing process of letting go. This doesn't mean you have to give up your job, friends, house, and possessions—it means you need to let go of any *attachments* you have toward them. Then, if they're not meant to be, they will naturally fall away. If they are meant for you, they will thrive in the space you've created for them.

When attachments dissolve, there's nothing to weigh you down. No one to hold you back. No expectations to feverishly fulfill. No stories to weld you to the past. You're free to be you. Once you have a regular deep breathing practice, you'll find yourself naturally more conscious and relaxed throughout the day. It's here in this languid state where you can openly and gladly surrender what needs to go and receive the cosmic goodness that wants to come in.

If you're chronically breathing short and shallow breaths, surrender will feel like torture; you'll be clinging to life as you know it to survive. Keep breathing, sweet Soul, and let it all go with the out breath.

How do you know what you're attached to? You'll know it because it's the thing you can't possibly do without, the person who's always on your mind (for better or worse), the outcome you absolutely have to have, the conversation that keeps on repeating, the stories you keep telling yourself and the world, the fears that keep you up at night, the insecurities that prevent you from living your dreams, the habit that you can't quit, the memory that you can't shake, the activity you obsess over, and all the labels and limits of your being.

These are your attachments.

But here's the thing … humans naturally have attachments because they have an ego. If you give yourself a hard time about your attachments, you're playing right into the ego's games. Surrender attachments without judgment. This doesn't mean you need to give your favorite jewelry away, ditch chocolate, and stop buying crystals. It simply means seeing life through the gently but powerfully unattached Soul rather than the hungrily attached and disempowered ego.

Just for a moment, imagine what that kind of life would look and feel like. Imagine letting go of old beliefs and ideas that have nothing to do with the life you want to create for yourself. Imagine living in a state of peaceful presence every day. Imagine being completely happy just *being alive*.

· PRACTICE ·
Releasing Attachments Soul Prompts

Without judgment, have a look at your attachments. Write down all the ones you can think of in a column. You might start with the objects at home that you're attached to, the people in your life who have upset you or you have upset, the aspects of your job that you feel strongly toward, the food you're craving every day, and perhaps the loudest thoughts. Resist labeling them as "good" or "bad," even in your mind; just write until they're all down. Next to each attachment, write (or say out loud) a powerful releasing statement that will set you free from them, one by one. You can create your own affirmations or try some of these:

- I am free to eat foods that nourish me.
- I choose friends who lift my spirits.
- I love myself and prioritize my well-being.
- I honor my heart's wisdom.
- I enjoy stillness and reveling in my unique presence.
- I release thoughts and beliefs that don't serve my highest good.
- I respect my body, mind, and Soul.
- I am grateful for Spirit's guidance, and I give thanks for all I have.
- I joyfully release any stories that perpetuate fear in my life.
- I lovingly let my ego's voice dissolve in my inner ocean of love.
- My blissful attitude makes me happier than anything I own.
- I naturally surrender all attachments that don't serve my greatest good.

Once you've created a list of affirmations, say them out loud every day for two weeks to fully charge their meaning into your whole self. Ensure you include the feeling of the affirmation beaming from your heart with every word. Then safely burn the pages and *let it all go*. If you don't wish to burn them, just release them energetically. You can, of course, create any ritual with these affirmations that suits you and allows for a more immersed state of surrender.

THERE'S NO SUCH THING AS LOST

I hear from many clients who admit they'd love to know themselves on a much deeper level, but perhaps when they're a bit more "spiritual," when they have more time, when the kids are older, when life isn't so chaotic, when they're not so scared of the unknown, or when they're not feeling so lost.

But there will never be a perfect time. You don't need to consider yourself "spiritual" to be able to know yourself on a deeper level. You will actually create more time and ease in your life when you are living with greater awareness. Children (yours or those around you) will benefit immensely from an intuitive carer. Life is always messy and chaotic; it's self-awareness that helps us navigate through the mess and back into feelings of serenity and contentment. The unknown is simply the Divine in motion, ready to take your hand. And lost is the very best place to start.

Although, you're never really lost. When you're feeling uncertain and hopeless and you don't know where to start, you've reached a powerful place to choose deep surrender. If you can allow yourself to surrender into this shadowy place of not-knowingness, confusion, and directionless wandering, then you won't feel lost for long. Here in your dark depths you can create a foundation for your future based on your Soul's power, purpose, and wisdom, rather than on someone else's advice. If you can surrender and tune inward, you'll find you're already home.

I've felt lost a hundred times in my life. Some of these moments have seen me on my knees, with tear-stained cheeks, palms turned upward, and a few words of surrender falling from my salty lips: "Hey, Great Spirit, I give up. Show me the way back onto my path. Love me and heal me and help me grow stronger every day. Strengthen my back, my bones, my wings, and my resolve. And so it is."

These are the uncomfortable, painful, squirmy moments that force me to give up what I think I know. I can see how pivotal and potent these moments are for my Soul's transformation. All because of surrender.

Slowly I'm learning to see the beauty while *in* the moment. That's a real gift. Smiling through tears. Gratitude during sleepless nights. Laughter in the midst of a truly hellacious day. Gravitating back to joy and trust when I've "failed" a hundred times.

So, feel lost, sweet Soul. Go on. Feel how that really feels for you. Take a moment to surrender the fight. Close your eyes. Ask your heart, *Where to now?* And when you're ready, take the first step.

If a step is too much for you right now, go ahead and rest. Have a nap in the shaded woods of your Soul. Nurture. Recover. Nourish. Heal. Surrender to whatever is happening. When you are strong enough, stand up and tune in. You've got this, warrior heart.

· RITUAL ·
A Prayer of Release

I've written this sacred prayer of release to be folded into your evening rituals as a way of surrendering from the day what is not meant for you. Trust that you are safe to let go and that this is creating space in your life for all that is good for your Soul. If you feel like it, add whatever words spill from your heart.

Surrender comes to me through breathing, poetry, prayer, songs, silence, humming, howling, tears, talking, drawing, and dancing. Every day requires surrender of some sort. Let it flow through you however it desires to.

> *Great Spirit, thank you for your infinitely comforting presence in my life. I ask that you come close to me now—allow*

*me to feel your powerful presence. Wrap me in layers of
golden light and fill me with unconditional love. Show me
how to surrender attachments to all people, places, objects,
thoughts, memories, energies, and substances that are not
aligned with my Highest Self. Dissolve and transmute anything from my energy field that does not belong to me. Heal
all parts of me that need restoration. Shine your cosmic
radiance into every fragment of my being so that I may feel
whole. Bless my life. My gratitude is eternal. And so it is.*

SOMETIMES LIFE INSISTS ON SURRENDER

It was May 2014. I was running late, but that was nothing new.
I was driving a familiar route to pick up my son from preschool. I
had left myself just enough time to buy some food from the shops
for dinner and return a package to a friend's house along the way.
I was happy, but frantic. My heart was racing. Music was blaring.
Thoughts were swirling like a storm. Nerves were on edge.

Suddenly I felt my left cheek go numb. I panicked. Was I having
a stroke? Then my left arm started to tingle. I thought for sure that
meant I was having a stroke. I was convinced I was, so I completely
freaked out.

I drove for a few tortuous minutes up the road before I noticed
a large pharmacy. I pulled into the parking lot. Sitting in the car, I
tried to convince myself that I was fine and I shouldn't be late for
school. But I wasn't fine. I was clearly the opposite of fine.

I got out of my car feeling helpless and panicked, and walked
into the pharmacy. Nervously, I headed to the back of the shop
where the pharmacists worked. I approached one of them, eyes
wide with panic, and whispered, "I think I'm having a stroke." He
looked at me with eyes of pure compassion, asked me to raise and
lower both of my arms, and then said, "You're not having a stroke.

You're okay." I told him my cheek was numb, my heart was racing, I felt dizzy, and I didn't know what to do. He asked me gently to sit down for a while, grabbed a cold bottle of water for me, and said he'd be back in a few minutes.

As I sat there, two elderly women with beautiful and strong crone presences sat down on either side of me. Without holding me, I felt held. Without saying a word, I felt understood. Without knowing why, I felt loved.

My numbness was subsiding, but the panic was pounding. I phoned my son's school and words about a "medical emergency" fell out of my mouth. I called my husband and asked him to pick up our son. Shortly after, the pharmacist came over to check on me, and after a brief conversation, he asked if I might be having a panic attack.

What now? No, no, no. I was sure this wasn't a panic attack. *This was real.* (Little did I know about panic attacks.) He smiled without patronizing me and said one of the other pharmacists was going to take me to the nearby medical center.

Half an hour later, I was sitting across from an exceptionally kind doctor who was explaining that the results from my electrocardiogram were normal, and it was highly likely I'd experienced a panic attack. The words felt heavier coming from her. They rolled around like large marbles in my head. *Panic attack. Panic. Attack.* "But I'm fine; I'm happy," I said.

She smiled. "How busy is your schedule?" she asked.

Still feeling edgy and vulnerable, I defensively blurted out a bunch of lies. I said it was "great" because I worked from home, which was so "easy," and I couldn't see why I would possibly have a panic attack.

She asked me to clear my calendar and actively look for ways to look after my body, mind, and Soul. I needed space to do nothing. *Nothing? Well, this is new to me…*

Since having my son, I hadn't created space to do nothing. Because motherhood, and work, and friends, and cleaning, and attachments to busy-ness were so strong, and oh my goodness the weeds in the garden were always so out of control. I couldn't remember the last time I'd surrendered to nothingness, to what my body needed, to deep nourishment.

Later that night in the bath, I cried. I began reflecting on what had happened so far that year. It was only May. In January, I'd had a devastating miscarriage. In March, my son had fallen from the top of a wall and narrowly escaped a head injury. And the week before, my husband and I had decided to plan a last-minute trip to San Francisco to visit friends. So much had happened, and I hadn't yet taken time out to properly grieve, heal, or recover from trauma and a really big scare. I just kept up the relentless pace. And planned a holiday. I had been fooling myself for years that working from home was easy. It wasn't *at all*.

Something inside me shifted. My defensiveness and lies were surrendered. The bathwater made space for saltwater as I wept for my body. I had taken it for granted, expecting it to carry out impossible feats every single day. I wept for my son, for his precious health. I wept for the baby we'd lost. I wept with gratitude for the state of panic that threw my whole life into disarray so that I could steadily find my center again. Because sometimes life insists.

That night I loved myself so hard. I breathed deeply. I took some grief-healing homeopathy. I listened to all the feelings. I opened up, softly, slowly, to what needed my attention. I surrendered the pain and let it speak. I surrendered my to-do list and created a self-love list. I surrendered what I thought was best for me and opened up to what was truly good for me. I surrendered my plans and let the Divine take the lead.

That night, I prayed to the universe that I would be shown an easier way, that I would understand what it felt like to live in accordance with my higher good, that I would know what it meant to cherish and adore myself every day.

Drying my tears, I whispered, "And so it is."

MAKING SPACE
FOR WILD, LOVING THOUGHTS

Surrendering unhelpful and unhealthy thoughts and beliefs will create space for bliss to bloom along your spiritual path. When you disable these kinds of thoughts...

- I'm not worthy of abundance.
- Love isn't for me.
- I'm not smart enough.
- No one wants to hear what I have to say.
- I have no real purpose or calling.
- I'm not special or talented.
- Life is so difficult.
- I have no choice but to stay stuck where I am.
- I'm not spiritual enough to be intuitive.

... and cultivate these kinds of thoughts...

- I was born worthy of greatness and endless abundance.
- Love is who I am and I accept it into my life in every way.
- I'm smart, brilliant, and witty in my own awesome way.
- I have so much to say, and I'm not afraid to share my thoughts.
- I open up to my Soul's purpose every day.

- I have gifts and I inspire others by simply being me.
- Life is beautiful, nourishing, and so good to me.
- I am free to create my life with every thought, word, action, and direction.
- I am a spiritual being and easily access my intuition daily.

…then you are actively believing in yourself and your Soul's guidance.

Surrender the negative, outdated thoughts to make space for new ones. Believe in your own inimitable greatness. The process is as easy as you allow it to be, so don't believe your ego when it makes up excuses to hold on to negative ways of thinking.

SURRENDER TO THE DIVINE

A part of the powerful practice of surrender is to relinquish the ego's control and give it over to the Divine, the universe, the radically loving powers that be, and the light within.

Each Soul is a unique and equal piece of the fabric of Great Spirit; we're all walking, talking Spirits in human bodies. Our Souls are love and light on a human journey.

Take a look at yourself for a moment through the eyes of your Soul. Eyes that are far more perceptive, eternal, and all-knowing. Eyes that aren't looking for flaws or any wrongdoing. Eyes that see the good, the beautiful, and the perfection in *all* of you. When you see yourself and your world this way, the hard edges soften, priorities shift, love flows in and out effortlessly, and surrender to bliss comes naturally.

When you know that inside of you and all around you lives a Soul of divine light that will never ask for too much, never make you do anything you don't want to do, you will realize that it is *here* you are safe. It is *here* in your own truth and presence you are home. It is *here* you are loved unconditionally.

Surrendering what isn't in alignment with your Soul is only ever painful if your ego has an almighty hold on it. The ego may cling desperately, telling you how much this stuff matters, that you need it, that it defines you, that without it you'll be a failure, lost, lonely, unhappy, regretful, and torn from what's best for you. Attachments are distractions, and the ego *loves* distractions. Yes, you need your people, food, clothes, water, shelter, and love. If you have these, you are blessed beyond measure. If you have anything extra, you are wildly abundant. But if you're attached to any of it, it won't bring you joy for long.

If you have too much stuff in your house to keep clean, if you have too much to do in your day, if you can't keep up with all your friends, if you feel drained, overwhelmed, and always on the run, stop and let go. Surrender the rush and competition. Notice the attachment and let it go. Create a life for yourself that's easy to live in a way that feels good and true for you. This way, you'll have easy access to love, light, and peace. This way, you'll always be home.

SPIRITUAL AND SPATIAL DECLUTTERING

I used to accumulate a lot of random, "meaningful" stuff. I once had a gorgeous collection of colored vintage glass vases. My husband spent years gathering unique European beer glasses. I bought cushion covers more often than I'd like to admit. I had cupboards full of teacups (for whom, I'm not so sure). I stocked drawers full of socks and jumpers I never wore, lined cupboards with board games we never played, filled bookshelves with books I would never read again, and picked up random knickknacks almost every time I went to a garage sale or a vintage shop.

Then I had kids. I suffered from anxiety and depression with both kids, and besides hugs, homeopathy, wholesome food, sunshine, and my incredible psychologist, shopping made me feel *so good*. My house was getting full, but it wasn't helping me at all. It was cluttering my home and my heart more and more. And the buzz I got from shopping didn't last long; it felt empty, echoey, and edgy.

Then one day, when my daughter was two, I was dusting my largely-ignored-but-perfectly-placed art deco vases when I had this overwhelming feeling of clarity and I wanted to scream, "Why do I have so much stuff?!"

Overnight I went from accumulation mode to decluttering queen. All the stuff without meaning, everything that wasn't being used or deeply cherished, and anything without practical necessity was sold or given away, and the thought of replacing it with more stuff repelled me.

Letting go of stuff requires the same strategy as letting go of unhealthy habits, behaviors, thoughts, expectations, stories, and people. For me, it goes like this:

1. Notice the attachment or the accumulation without judgment.

2. See the attachment as merely an ego-driven thought that can be dissolved at any time.

3. Be willing to let go of the attachment.

4. Open your heart and let go.

5. Thank it for what it has brought to your life or taught you.

6. Know that you are safe and lighter without it.

7. Rediscover the art of appreciating a sweet moment without trying to own it.

As you get into a surrender practice on a physical level, you'll begin to notice space in your home. Initially you might freak out, wondering what you'll replace the old items with. You might also lean toward guilt for buying the pieces, books, toys, dishes, clothes, or other stuff in the first place. Be kind to yourself; you were and are doing the best you can. Surrender the need to fill the space and any guilt that arises. Space in your home allows for a more fluid flow of energy, which impacts the state of your mind and heart.

Eventually you'll see limited options as an advantage. Less in your home means less stress, less time cleaning, and a clearer mind. Everything that's left will be genuinely meaningful. Your body will respond with more serenity and comfort. The effect will ripple out through your whole life.

If you're an extrovert, try holding a garage sale. If you're more introverted, sell your stuff online. Or just give it away. Cease clinging, and the universe will show you what to do.

Make Room for Magic

When you create a life with sacred space and leisurely moments of time set aside to be still, you're not doing nothing, you're actively *being*—a truly profound way to live. Surrendering to stillness may seem like wasting time at first, but eventually you'll see shifts in your life.

These shifts might feel magical, like stretching time, grasping insights, feeling indescribable joy, or tapping into wild self-love. Or they may feel uncomfortable if the space that you open up to is asking you to release, heal, or renew and you're resisting what needs to be done. Stillness and space sound so easy to embrace, but for many they're not because of fear of the unknown and the uncertainty of change.

We're a culture that craves comfort, shopping, noise, entertainment, amusement, food, alcohol, screens, social media, and all things bright, loud, activating, numbing, and distracting. We fill our homes with trinkets that are empty of meaning. We pile high the magazines that tell us we're not good enough. We fill our fridges, pantries, wardrobes, cupboards, beauty cabinets, garages, sheds, bookshelves, and spare drawers with stuff. We shove stuff under our beds and over our heads. We save things for the future because we haven't surrendered our past.

This fake sense of comfort that we derive from material possessions is always a reflection of what's going on in our precious minds and hearts. Repetitive, negative thoughts. Old stories. Out-of-date ideals. Perfect expectations. Stifled emotions. Other people's views. Everything saved ... just in case. Everything valued ... because who are we without it?

All this stuff we simply don't need, and deep down don't actually want, is holding us back from a life of true abundance. Yet we hold on tightly not just to the stuff, but to the endless thoughts and feelings that play constantly. The old stories give us comfort. The ideals give us a false sense of purpose. The stifled emotions keep us from healing and changing. The victim mentality provides something to solve. The expectations give us an unfounded feeling of control.

When we hoard these outdated thoughts and emotions in our minds, when our brains are wall-to-wall junk, we leave no room for magic. No space for creativity. No open window to let the stardust in. No chance to discover who we are underneath it all. We *need* magic. Without it, we are carbon-copy, suppressed and repressed, frustrated and hollow humans, following other people, chasing someone else's dreams, never taking a deep, deliciously full breath or thinking for our own wild selves.

Magic is the result of surrendering to stillness and allowing self-awareness to bloom in fortuitous ways.

It's not always easy to surrender life to a divine order, to your Soul's path, to silence, to the unknown. Living free and wild is a bold thing to do. But without space, there's no finding your true self in the center of your sacred, eternal being. Underneath the dust and the debris is the real you and your treasured truth.

Clutter, no matter where it lives, needs to be cleared out bit by bit. Slowly, but deliberately, the pieces and the stories are taken out the door. It seems an impossible task when you've accumulated so much stuff. But it's possible. Believe me, it's possible.

When you meditate, you're clearing out the mental clutter. Just one minute a day is a brilliant, I mean *brilliant* place to start if you've never meditated before. When you breathe consciously, you're tuning in to your sacred body and coming out of your head-space. You're finding yourself and detaching from your cluttering thoughts. When you take an inventory of your emotions with a psychologist, a friend, or your journal, you're able to witness what is taking up space and clouding your well-being. When you surrender expectations and have faith that the universe will provide all you need, miracles happen. When you say, *"Enough, I'm done,"* to the stories that keep replaying, you kick out the old furniture of beliefs, rearrange the few valued pieces, and, suddenly, you have much more space to dance.

Truly, it is a dance.

Surrendering to life is clearing a dance floor for magic to come alive. As you let go, you learn to open to the space you have cleared. When you surrender to nothingness and silence, your own song will come to life, your heart will know the steps, and luminosity will burst from your being.

Space Clearing Soul Prompts

Make a plan to help you uncover more of the mental, emotional, and physical stuff that needs to be taken out of your life. Write down some dates when you will have a garage sale, make a big delivery to a thrift or charity store, or create simple daily reminders that will encourage you along the way. Ask for help if you need it from friends and family. Here are some questions to open your mind and your life to deeper clarity.

Where have you accumulated unnecessary physical stuff? Where do you hide things in your house or car? Where does stuff naturally build up? How does it make you feel?

How will you begin or continue the clearing process of your home? Put aside ten minutes each day and devote that time to one room until it feels peaceful, then move on to the next room. Get conscious of each cupboard instead of ignoring the clutter behind closed doors. Have a garage sale and let the unloved pieces go in one day. Ask your friends what they do with their unwanted pieces.

What old beliefs are keeping you trapped? Outdated beliefs may include thoughts around your body, hair, career, partner, or home that have come from family members, early caregivers, or partners. Consciously and gently open your ears to the thoughts that arise. If they're love-based and feel like your truth, then they're aligned and helpful, whether they came from within you or somewhere else. If they're fear-based or simply don't feel like you, they're probably beliefs from someone else. Without judgment, surrender them. Take a deep breath and say, "This is not my truth." Create a new belief that sounds like love and truth.

What repetitive thoughts are you willing to let go of? Are you ready to let go of thoughts about your body or appearance that aren't positive? Can you drop the thoughts that don't support a more aware and enlightened life? Are you prepared to look at people without judgment, only compassion? What else comes up for you?

What unhelpful or unhealthy emotions do you need help with? Repetitive and strong emotions—such as anger, depression, anxiety, harsh self-criticism, or deep sadness—that are uneasy or negative are necessary to release whenever you become aware of them. Feel them, open to them, and let them go.

What ego clutter is getting in the way of your spiritual practice? The ego will tell you that the rituals you love are a waste of time, too hard, not worth it, boring, or empty. Whenever you notice this, you are more able to surrender these thoughts and the accompanying emotions from the ego and rise above them. Then take time to connect to your Highest Self and align with your Soul's truth.

Where do you feel the most serene? What does this place look like? How can you infuse the energy of this space into the rest of your world? If there's a particular place in nature that creates a sense of beauty and light in your being, find a way to place reminders around your home that have the same energy. This way, bliss is always in reach.

Three Pillars of Surrender

When I think about surrender, there are three qualities that feel the most important to me: pausing, stillness, and mindfulness. At first, they may sound remarkably similar, but each has its own intricate qualities, and individually they have had an enormously positive effect on my life as I've come to appreciate and open to surrender.

Pausing. Before you make a decision, race out the front door, make a large purchase, call someone important, start work on a project, or do anything significant, take a minute to pause and center yourself. Take a deep breath and tune in to your heart. This ensures you're not always on the run with a frantic mind. This creates a moment to listen to the quiet within. The more you pause, the more you hear.

Stillness. Whenever you can, be still. Relax. Get comfortable. Wake up slowly. Find peace in everyday moments with the people you love. Put your phone away. Enjoy the view. In stillness, you surrender busy-ness and multitasking and open to receive. In stillness, you find yourself.

Mindfulness. Be present in your life. Use your senses to experience your day. Pay gentle attention to what's going on around and within you. Be aware of all of it but attached to nothing. Gently bring your mind back when it wanders into the future or the past. Connect to that which opens you up to a higher way of being and living.

With pausing, stillness, and mindfulness, you'll easily come back in tune with your heart's rhythm and truth.

ABANDONING THE EGO'S FEARS

The ego is a fear-breeding, sneaky little voice. It wants to keep you small and stuck, so whenever you consider trying something new, it will come at you with a thousand fearful—but apparently "logical"—reasons why you should definitely not try new ideas, take on exciting adventures, or ever, ever believe in yourself as a person worthy of transformation and greatness.

When you learn to regularly drop into your heartspace and tune in to the loving sound of your Soul, you will realize that your ego is definitely not you. Your ego's fears are not your fears. Your ego's childish, critical, arrogant, and whiney voice is *so not you*. It's up to you to abandon the ego's fears as soon as they emerge, to stay as high as your Soul's true vibrations, to sync with the pace of love, and to allow all flavors of abundance to flow into your life.

Surrendering the ego is an endless practice that will raise your energy higher and higher the more you keep letting it go.

When you hear fear-driven thoughts arise from your ego's voice, stay in a loving mindset, surrender the urge to play along with it, and say, "Hey ego, I know what game you're playing, and I'm going to lovingly and firmly ask that you keep your voice down. Yes, we're transforming. Yes, we're trying something new. Yes, it's going to be awesome, even if we feel wobbly or mess it up. Yes, we're safe. Thank you for leaning toward the light with us. All is well."

Can you sense how gently optimistic and brave it feels to say this out loud? Your ego is not to be ignored or shut down (an impossible task). It's to be taken under your wings and shown a more expansive view. If you can surrender your ego's fears every moment they arise, they will eventually have less influence in your life, and this space will allow for positivity and love. Just open your heart and let go.

MINDFULNESS IN THE MESSY MOMENTS

During the months following my son's birth in 2010, I journeyed into a dark and lonely place. I suffered postnatal depression and intense anxiety, so I was basically never present to the moment. I truly had no idea what was happening to me. I was tired right down to my bones. I had isolated myself from everyone I loved—including those I lived with. I was feeling guilty for bringing my boy into the world through an emergency caesarean. I was feeling lonely in a new neighborhood. One day I'd be overcome with rage; the next, complete despair. I had dangerous thoughts, and I didn't know what to do with them. I was trying desperately to control my messy life, but the less I surrendered to it, the more intense my inner struggle became.

Thankfully, I found an incredible psychologist to talk to, and my naturopath prescribed some calming and healing supplements. My body felt nourished and my emotions felt lighter. The light was peeking through and pulling me toward it like a love magnet.

At some point, I picked up a book called *Buddhism for Mothers*, by Sarah Napthali. I was hungry for her wisdom daily. Each night after my boy went to sleep, I'd curl up with this book and read it until my eyes hurt. Slowly, the lessons and stories began to infuse their ease into my frazzled mind—like lavender in a warm bath—and unwind my anxiety from the inside out. A slow and necessary process of surrender was taking place, and as I loosened my grip, life found me again.

Sarah had a powerful way of gently guiding me toward awareness of the present moment. She showed me that even with small children and mental illness, real joy was possible. She spoke of mindfulness in the mundane and joy in the simplicity of life.

I was often angry and resentful of the jobs that had to be done around the house. I'd wash the dishes, hang up the clothes, clean the bathroom, and wash the floor with such disdain because the *only* thing I wanted to be doing when my boy napped was rest (and read). I was fighting against life itself, resisting everything that was right in front of me, and losing the battle daily.

I remember the night it all changed for me. I was hanging laundry on the washing lines outside after settling my boy in bed. My hands unexpectedly came alive, and I began to feel—I mean *really, sensually feel*—the wet texture of each item. I put them to my cheek and gave thanks for the clothes, my family, and my life. I surrendered to and fell in love with the moment, and it was such bliss.

The next day, I mindfully took to washing the dishes. I simply and gratefully connected with the warm, soapy water on my skin. Plates, bowls, and cutlery slipped through my hands. I finally stopped detesting it and embraced it for what it was: a blessing in disguise.

I found the more I surrendered into mindfulness without forcing it, the more my life became positive, wholehearted, and happy again. Happy in a way I hadn't felt in so long. Absolutely nothing in my life had changed, but the way I saw it had transformed. Life was playing out before me, and I had two choices: surrender into it or rally against it.

I completely fell in love with mindfulness, and by mindfulness, I mean life. And when I held my boy, my sweet, beautiful baby boy, I was finally able to just *be* with him, love him, find peace with him, and surrender to each unpredictable moment.

Life didn't suddenly become perfect and easy. Motherhood is a rough ride. Moving house is tricky. Depression is dark. Anxiety is intense. My mind and body still had so much to heal. But as I accepted and surrendered to what was in front of me, my life brightened, and I've never been to such a dark place since.

These days, I find myself learning mindfulness on a whole new level. Our daughter is five years old. She's smart, determined, and completely gorgeous, but her stubborn attitude and wild ways have tested my mindfulness and resolve. I am far from flawless, but that's hardly the point. What matters is that I am conscious of my actions and reactions, thoughts and emotions, judgments and expectations, and if I'm courageous enough, I can let them all go and simply be mindful to what is.

Mindfulness during an intense tantrum is a surprisingly beautiful thing. I don't have to know the reason for her upset, nor do I need to fix it; all I need to do is be there for her, in whatever capacity I have available. Some days, I'm so in tune with that level of surrender; other days, I lose my footing. I'm not proud of how I've reacted at times, but the softer I become—with self-love, self-care, boundaries, and healing—the easier it is to let go and be present.

Mindfulness is the best gift you can give yourself and the treasured people in your life. And it's the only way to be completely, clearly, and consciously self-aware. When you are in tune with life, you are in tune with your body, your senses, your energy, your spirit, and how every part of you is dancing together, journeying through life. Gently pay attention to life's precious moments. They're all we've got.

· Practice ·
Mindful Magic Soul Prompts

No matter where you're at along your mindfulness journey, there are ways to seep into the moment, however that looks right now. Let your body sink into the chair, floor, or ground a little. Take a deep breath and surrender any tension in your muscles. Look at what is happening around you without judgment or commentary. Don't let your ego tell you this is difficult; that's a story that simply isn't true. If you're curious about mindfulness, try opening up to your truth with the following questions, either in a journal or as you meditate on the idea of what mindfulness means to you.

What is it about this moment that feels good? How exactly does it feel? Describe in as much detail as possible; really submerge into the moment.

Does anything feel uncomfortable? Why is it uneasy? What does that tell you? How can you surrender this feeling?

How can you lean into a little more mindfulness? How can you surrender your day and fully appreciate what is happening for you right now? How can you take in your world more deeply through your senses? How can you be more present for what truly matters to you?

SACRED AND PLEASURABLE RITUALS

The beauty of leisurely and pleasurable rituals is that they provide a nurturing basis for your spirituality, a touchpoint during busy days to come home to yourself. Rituals are a loving way to honor yourself and all that is sacred to you, deepening your connection to self and Spirit. They're the heartbeats of life, providing a mindful, soothing, and meaningful rhythm. Rituals cultivate an awareness that goes beyond everyday living into the heart and Soul of what matters most. By surrendering busy-ness and creating stillness and pauses, you'll find you have more time to open up to rituals that bring you closer to the mystery of all that you are.

You may wish to try the following rituals at the same time each day or week or simply flow between them whenever feels good.

· RITUAL ·
Sunrise Prayer for Surrender

With these or your own words, say a prayer that opens your heart to gratitude, surrenders your thoughts into the arms of positivity, and fills your whole being with joy. Write it down and stick it somewhere you'll see every day.

As you say the following words out loud, feel them move through your body. As you feel what kindness, generosity, divine love, protection, and humility feel like, they will come to life in your energy field and expand through your life. Say this prayer and, if you feel so called, write your own in your journal.

Thank you, Great Spirit, for another day in this breathtaking body. Thank you for my health, happiness, and the many gifts of today. Show me how to be kind and generous. Fill me with wonder, inspiration, and direction. Guide me toward fulfilling my Soul's true desires. Surround me with your love and light. Help me to be of service to all. Wrap me up in your flawless protection and let me be firm in my boundaries and integrity. I am humbled to be your warrior, a lightworker of peace and compassion. I surrender to whatever is good and right for my Highest Self. And so it is.

· Ritual ·
Mother Earth Meditation

Lie down on a gorgeous patch of Mother Earth somewhere you won't be disturbed. On the days you can't do this outside—if you don't have the energy or the weather isn't right for adventuring out—try it in your bed while picturing a blissful scene in nature.

Begin with plenty of luscious, deep breaths. Gradually think of each part of your body, from the top of your head to the tips of your toes, and gently relax each part, surrendering them directly into Mother Earth's healing hands. Visualize or feel this happening slowly, vividly. Start with the crown of your head, then forehead, eyes, nose, lips, teeth, jaw, cheeks, ears, neck, shoulders, arms, hands, back, chest, belly, hips, legs, and feet. Take your time moving all the way down. Sink into this healing sensation. Feel your whole body release and surrender as one. Melt your fears, concerns, and worries into nature's energy; let them dissolve.

If you're in bed, this is a good time to fall asleep. If you're outside, gently come back into your body with soft stretches. Stand up slowly when you're ready.

· RITUAL ·
Create a Sacred Altar

Let your heart guide you toward the best place in your home for an altar. Choose a table, trunk, ledge, or other flat surface. Set an intention for the altar. You might like to have one for calling in abundance, honoring the seasons, connecting with ancestors, expressing joy, or receiving guidance. Start by placing one or two key pieces in the center. Over the following days or weeks, gradually add to it.

You can place anything you want on your altar. I like crystals, oracle cards, feathers, candles, shells, jewelry, statues, coins, and other meaningful bits and pieces from around my home and the world. Keep it clean. Acknowledge it every day. Change it around as often as your heart wants to. Give thanks for the connection and clarity it brings to your life. Honor yourself for this beautiful and sacred devotional practice.

When you sit with your altar, choose a ritual that speaks to you. It may be burning sage and singing, meditating and praying, surrendering your concerns, playing a drum or singing bowl, or just sitting with a particular crystal and receiving energy. It doesn't matter what it is; it matters how it makes you feel. Surrender a small amount of time each day to sit with your altar, and the rest of your day will be so much more pleasurable, sacred, and productive.

· RITUAL ·
Colorful Therapy

Writing and art therapy are uniquely healing ways to allow your Soul to communicate with you through words, emotions, thoughts, ideas, color, and form. Doodling or drawing in your journal is a creative way to delve deep into your intuition alongside the powerful use of words. Your intuition doesn't use words and loves to be expressed in other ways. Art is a perfect way to do this.

When drawing, use as much color as you can and don't attempt to make sense of the art as you make it. Surrender completely to the process. Surrender your not-creative-enough beliefs, surrender your inner critic and editor, and surrender the need to make it perfect. The mind will be tempted to analyze and critique it, but try to keep these thoughts quiet. When it's complete, you can make sense of it—if you want to—by asking yourself what you feel it's all about. The main purpose is soulful expression, to surrender to the artist within, but if there's something else to be gained, then your experience will be all the richer.

Deeply and Divinely Protected

Shiny, Soul-driven people are enormously attractive. When you're aligned with your Highest Self and living an abundant and aware life, people will want to be with you, but not all of them will have the right intentions.

I've had some intense experiences with unfavorable energies, but from these incidents I have learned so much about taking care of my energy. My focus is always love, not fear of what might happen. Keep love as your filter, your anchor, and your focus while maintaining big, strong boundaries.

I believe protection is a result of the process of surrender, because when I surrender my fears about the world and the people in it, I step into a new way of living that resonates with and attracts only love. It's in this space where I feel oneness, where negative and harmful energies—based on separation—can't reach me.

I use a daily ritual of opening to love that naturally protects my being from negative energies, and a weekly ritual for clearing my energy and raising my vibration. Consciously looking after yourself each day assists with the process immensely, but if you drink excessive alcohol, obsess over social media, spend hours staring at a screen, gossip or judge incessantly, or otherwise lower your vibes, then you're also lowering your energetic defenses. These defenses may also crumble when you are overwhelmed, grieving, sick, or otherwise energetically depleted. Your power stays strong when you are healthy, responsible, grounded, and anchored into love. There will be times when your energy is low; this is your body saying it needs comfort, love, or something else unique to your needs. If you are moving through a difficult or dark time, extend your meditations and prayers longer every day. Surrender and give in to being still and present to your Soul's needs.

When your energy is low, negativity can edge in. So while it's important to trust in divine protection, it's also really smart to be responsible for your own energy. Clean up your energetic field at least once a week and see an energy healer if you need assistance.

· Ritual ·
Morning Love Visualization

Sit up in bed when you first wake up. Breathe deeply and take your time with this process. Let your Soul's light expand to fill your whole being. Feel your energetic roots sinking into Mother Earth, deep, deep down into the earth's core. Feel your crown chakra opening while golden white light pours through your crown and bathes your inner body with pure healing. Allow the doors of your heart to open wide and imagine unconditional love flowing in and out. Send love to all your favorite people, your Spirit Guides, animals, your home, and anything or anyone else who comes into your heart. Send love to your community, country, and all over the globe. Now receive love from everyone and everything you've just imagined. Allow love to flow into the depths of your being. Fill yourself completely with divine love. Feel love flowing effortlessly in and out of your being, touching all the areas and problems of your life, alchemizing everything that's dark or heavy into love and light. Surrender all blocks to love. Know in your being that love is the most protective force of all. Keep breathing and allow messages or visions to come through. When you feel this process is complete, thank the Divine, the Source of all love and protection, and slowly open your eyes. And so it is.

· RITUAL ·
Weekly Clearing Visualization

Lie down somewhere comfortable and allow your whole body to sink into whatever is beneath you. Surrender your worries. Breathe deeply. Take a few moments to receive bright healing light throughout your body. When you feel relaxed and aware of your energetic state, ask your Soul to show you anything that you need to clear and surrender in your mind, body, spirit, or surroundings. You may feel that a particular chakra is depleted and asking for deeper healing. You may notice a part of your house or car that needs energetic cleansing. You might hear the name of a healer or friend whom you are being called to check in with. You might see a vision of something you've been obsessing over that you need to mentally let go of. Your inner senses will show you what you need to clear and surrender. Whenever something arises, simply send it healing and love and feel the profound freedom this brings to your being. When you are complete, imagine a cloud of perfect white light surrounding you, bringing you peace and wholeness. Thank Great Spirit and anyone else you may have sensed was present and helping you with these insights. Gently stretch and be present in your body.

Take your time with these meditations. Feel into them and try them your way. Trust that your Highest Self knows what needs to be done. As you expand your self-awareness, your light will shine brighter than ever, sweet Soul. Don't let fears of unworthiness or negativity dim your light. Surrender them to the Divine. You have nothing to fear, for you are always only surrendering back to love.

Expansive Sense of Self

Deep breaths and surrender create space—if you're generous with yourself, lots of space—to clear out the seemingly endless self-talk from your mind, to soften into your wise and sensual body, to open your heart to the outpourings of love all around you, and to surrender to the guidance from your Soul.

Every time you consciously surrender, you're able to expand your sense of self. Your sense of self is how you perceive yourself, how much self-confidence you have, how deeply you trust yourself, and the beliefs that come from within.

Journaling will give you powerful insights into your sense of self. So will following your dreams, taking responsibility for your energy, valuing your gifts, making decisions based on how aligned you feel, and healing your past. There are so many ways to get to know the true you.

All of these require some form of surrender for them to happen fully and completely. When you consciously begin the process of surrender, it may feel intense or awkward. Keep trying. Put loving reminders all over your house. Play peaceful music in the car. Declutter all the spaces. Say no to the things that don't feel right. Make time in your diary for play and meditation. Love and acknowledge yourself every single time you do this.

Slow, soulful living is all about coming back to your truth, the only guidance you'll ever need. When you rush, you have the tendency to follow others. When you bring in mindfulness, you have the power to align with yourself.

Try spending just one day getting to know yourself anew through slow surrender. Speak to yourself kindly and use affirmations like the ones that follow. Build up your confidence through conscious decisions. Look for ways in which you make a difference. Expand your sense of self by taking up more energetic space in the world.

· RITUAL ·
Affirmations for Surrender

Use these affirmations—or create your own with positive and inspiring words—to bring a deeper level of surrender into your world. Say out loud what feels supple and untethered to you. Write them on a piece of paper and stick them where you'll notice them every day.

- I am free to be all me in this moment.
- I joyfully claim my inner desires and divinity.
- I am grateful for the support of the universe wherever I go.
- I allow my body to completely relax.
- I accept whatever I'm feeling now and release it.
- I welcome who I am in this moment without judgment.
- I surround myself with people who understand and appreciate me.
- I use my gifts each day to infuse the world with my light.
- I surrender into bliss.

· PRACTICE ·
Complete Surrender Soul Prompts

As we wrap up this section on surrender, let's look at inspired ways that you can stretch into surrender. Find a place to relax and open your heart. Finish these sentences with an honest and loving answer. Say them out loud or write them down.

- The last time I fully relaxed was when …
- My mind feels most awake and aware when I am …
- How I feel when I surrender busy-ness is …
- Today I choose to slow down by …
- In this moment, I am ready to release …
- Rituals that help me surrender into peace are …
- Habits that no longer give me the joy I crave are …
- Today, my intuition asked me to …
- Each time I surrender into my magnificence, I am able to …

When this process is complete, give thanks to your inner wisdom.

Chapter 6
CONNECT

*"At any moment, you have a choice that either leads you
closer to your spirit or further away from it."*
—THICH NHAT HANH

Connecting to the wild wisdom within is so vitally important; without this connection, we feel lost, broken, unsure, unsteady, or afraid. With a deep connection to love, we feel a kindred communion with ourselves and Spirit, we are informed and guided from the highest possible source, and we come back home to ourselves. Let's look at ways to connect to self first, then we'll get to know what connecting with Spirit looks like.

CONNECT TO YOUR INIMITABLE SELF

Along my journey into self-awareness, I've consciously deepened my connection both to myself and to Spirit. Both matter. Connecting to the universe within will teach you about the universe all around you, while discovering more about the cosmic universe around you will mirror and inform what's on the inside, too.

THE WONDER OF YOU

When you've cultivated a sacred practice of deepening your breath and surrendering what no longer aligns, you've created a portal to connect to the one thing that will nourish and guide you from a place of unfailing love … your inner spirit.

As you connect deeply with yourself through curiosity, compassion, acceptance, and love, you'll create an unshakable foundation for an empowered life. It's both rock-hard and yet completely malleable, giving you a feeling of security from deep within that is still continuously able to bend and flow with life. This connection is formed with self-inquiry, held together with formidable self-belief, and, through devotion to mindfulness and conscious living, can withstand any storm. Nothing can shake you, and no one can blow you over when you've developed and strengthened this connection to yourself.

It's time to listen to your heart, lovingly face your fears and shadows, embrace your sensitivities, deepen your roots, and open yourself up to the wonder of all that you are. Let's connect.

DEEPEN YOUR CONNECTION

Here are three simple meditations to connect you specifically to each of your wisdom guides. I've created these to be as effortless as possible so that you're able to connect to them at any time and place and add your own flavor to each. As best you can, find a place where you won't be disturbed, and have your notebook close by.

· RITUAL ·
Insightful Meditation

The meditation that follows was created to deepen your connection to insights from your Highest Self and the divine wisdom within and around you. Insights can be difficult to welcome when you're lying down (the neocortex gets sleepy in this position), so I encourage you to find a comfortable way to stand up for this meditation, such as while walking in nature. Standing up awakens your brain and body, creating a flow of wisdom through you. You can receive insights with your eyes open, but if you're finding it difficult, try resting up against a tree with your eyes closed. Start by reciting this affirmation: *I am always connected to my spirit, and I easily receive insights when I need them or when they desire to find me.*

Now, imagine the tip of your energy field—slightly above the top of your head—slowly opening like a flower, petal by petal. Imagine the color of the flower, any color that comes to mind, then the shape of the petals, and the way they gracefully unfold. Visualize rainbow light pouring in through the center of your flower, the crown of your head. Feel this light move all the way through you and pour out of your feet into the ground beneath you. Focus on being receptive to the intelligent, creative, and mystical guidance of Spirit moving through you.

Ask your Highest Self to be present in your field of energy and open to any insights from here. Take your time with this connection. Trust that this is coming from the highest expression of your Soul. Next, ask Spirit a specific question and then remain silent and patient while the answer comes to you. You may see a being of light, hear words or a voice, notice signs or symbols, recognize an idea or a solution to a problem, or sense the message in another way that is unique and perfect for you. If you don't receive a response immediately, trust that the answer will unfold in your life soon.

Breathe deeply. Surrender the doubt. Connect to love. Allow insight to come to you. Take your time with this meditation; it will get easier the more you practice it.

You'll know when you have received an insight by the uplifting effect it has on your body and because it will be new information or known information put together in a new way. Allow your mind to creatively receive what you need to know.

When you feel you are done, give thanks for all you've received and write down your insights in your notebook. It may not make sense straight away; just note down what you experienced in faith that, eventually, it will.

· Ritual ·
Intuitive Meditation

This wholehearted meditation was designed to help you receive loving guidance from your intuition as you connect to your heartspace. It's best to practice this ritual in a seated position, as this is the easiest way for your body to access intuitive guidance. When you are seated or kneeling, you activate the limbic brain. You can access your intuition in any state, but to give this meditation the best chance of flowing, it's best to avoid lying completely flat or standing. Start by reciting this affirmation: *I am always connected to my wise heart and open to unlimited intuitive feedback for my highest good.*

Place your hands gently on your heartspace. Breathe deeply, allowing your belly and chest to fill completely before exhaling gently, slowly, from your mouth. Soften your heart and give thanks for the life it gives you. Be completely present in the moment and connected to what your heart wants to share with you. Allow it to come in any way that is right for you, be it as a feeling, an emotion, a song, a vibration, an energy, a vision, or a loving release.

Your heart may want to guide you intuitively in a specific area or situation of concern, or it may want to connect you to a higher state of peace and bliss. It may want you to feel the inner warmth of self-love and compassion, or it may show you how brilliant and creative you are. Stay open to the process as it will be unique for you and may change each time.

Breathe deeply. Allow intuition to flow through and all around you. Expect the unexpected. Ask questions. Take your time. You are intuitive, you are connected, and you are eternally wise. Slowly open your eyes when you are complete.

Give thanks to your immensely wise heart for all you've received and write down your intuitive messages in your notebook.

· RITUAL ·
Instinctive Meditation

This meditation was designed to ground you and help you feel safe. As you're accessing your ancient instinct and unconscious information, lying down is the perfect pose to activate and heal your reptilian brain and the guidance within. Start by saying this affirmation: *I am always safe, loved, and protected. The universe has a sacred place for me. I welcome instinctive feedback from my happy, healthy belly. All is well.*

Lie down somewhere comfortable. Soften your belly as it expands with the in breath, and allow your whole body to soften with the out breath as you relax every bone, every organ, every muscle, every cell, and every thought. Trust that you are held wholly by Mother Earth. Breathe deeply as you ground your energy, melding your vibration with nature's energy from above and below.

Place both hands on your belly, fill it with love, and surrender any fears that you feel arise. Keep breathing. Trust that you are safe. Relax the muscles on your face. Allow your instinct to open up to you with every breath. Ask your instinct questions if you desire. You may receive images of people, places, or situations that you need space from, or you may simply feel a release and healing.

Send your instinct love and healing. Envisage a vibrant and soothing soft red light around your belly, healing your connection to the earth, to ancestors, to your family, and to your childhood. Visualize yourself feeling safe and secure wherever you go. If anything feels uncomfortable, let Great Spirit heal and transmute it into love instantly.

Take your time with this meditation; enjoy the feeling of security and deep love. Give thanks to your instinct for all you've received and write down your thoughts in your notebook. Rest for as long as you need to.

LOVE IS THE ENERGY OF CONNECTION

You are love. Your spirit is love in motion. Let love in. Let love out. Open your heart to experience love's healing powers. And when you do, love will quench the deep thirst of your entire being.

Anytime you desire to experience the sacred and wild energy of love within you, close your eyes and connect to yourself on a Soul level where pure love is always present—your Soul has no fear.

Divine love is the strongest force that you could ever experience. It is magnificent, undiluted, healing, spirited, always available, and infinitely enduring. It goes beyond words; it's the deepest feeling and guidance of all. When you let love become your superpower, you open yourself up to a miraculous life. When you open the floodgates to love, you gently, compassionately, and powerfully transmute everything based in fear into love. The ego becomes your ally. Your thoughts are powerfully positive. Your emotions are free to move because all is welcome inside love.

When you connect to the vibration of love, you're connecting to the intelligence of consciousness and to your own ancient knowing. Love is what made the universe and what keeps it spinning. Love is the voice of Great Spirit and all Spirits of the higher dimensions who guide you. Love is the glue that holds all the goodness together. And love is the voice of your Soul, your inner knowing, your Highest Self.

When you realize that you are love and that your intuition is simply the loving and gentle feeling nudging you toward your greatness, you'll realize, too, that you've heard this voice before. This isn't new. What's new is that you're now open and ready to hear and honor it in a whole new way.

Love is quiet and heartfelt. It's the underlying strength throughout your life, whispering words of devotion, like these:

- You're okay.
- You've got this.
- You can do anything.
- You are so kind.
- You are making a difference.
- You are healing.
- Take as much time as you need.

Fear is all around, too. If you buy into fear, that gives the ego permission to keep you stuck—never changing, never growing, never evolving. The ego is wired by fear, fueled by separation, drunk on unworthy thoughts, and not fit to rule your life.

The ego will beg you to play small, shame you into feeling bad, and plunge you into guilt for what's gone "wrong" in your life. The ego will try to sound clever and will no doubt try these on:

- That's not going to work because in the past you messed it up.
- Don't even try because everyone else is better than you.
- You haven't got the confidence/talents/qualifications to pull that off.

- It's much easier to stay small because you'll fail anyway.
- You're not worthy of that kind of success.
- Changing your life will mess everything up.
- Self-awareness is too hard; we don't need to know what we don't already know.

As you become more conscious of and caring for your thoughts, they will naturally soften, and you'll begin to identify with the quiet voice of your heart. If you're not sure where the voice that you hear is coming from, check in to see if it is coming from love or fear by how it feels in your body.

Every thought has a unique vibration. This energy will affect your whole being. When you think a loving thought or create a love-based emotion, you'll feel sweet and light all over. Notice this feeling. Connect to it deeply.

When you think a fearful thought or create a fear-based emotion, you'll feel uncomfortable, restrictive, or heavy. Whenever you have this reaction, check in to see where your thoughts were headed. Was the ego trying on a lie? Were you repeating someone else's idea as your own? Notice this feeling. It's not your truth. Let it wash away with a deep breath.

When your inner compass points to love, the lens with which you see the world will change. You'll find peace in the raw truth of who you are. You'll experience the joy of transformation. You'll feel responsibility without guilt, anger without shame, frustration without attachment, and sadness without misery. You'll feel empowered to do something about your situation, the people around you, and the world as a whole. You'll see that your truth is as perfectly formed, fluid, and valuable as anyone else's. You'll see miracles on every street corner, in the hearts of the people you meet, and in acts of kindness. You'll notice that nothing is a coincidence. You'll see how breathtaking it is to be alive.

Connecting with the world through love is neither ignorant nor naïve. It's smart. It's intuitive. It's how we were designed. It's the only way I know to be happy, content, and free.

As you develop your self-awareness, you'll become so self-loving, self-compassionate, self-motivated, and self-made that you'll be a beacon for others. People will want to be with you, ideas will flow through you, guidance will be easily available, and alignment will always be in reach.

Connect only to love.

· PRACTICE ·
Self-Connection Soul Prompts

If your ego has been running the show lately, it might feel like a big leap to embrace radically loving thoughts. Start small and stay true. Answer the following questions while tuning in to your authentic self through the spirit of love. Choose one and write as much as you can or choose them all. If you'd prefer not to write the answer, write the question that speaks the most to you on a piece of paper and post it somewhere obvious. Let the answers flow through your heart as you go about your day.

How does love feel in your body?

If love had a message for you right now, what would it be?

What does your body want to say today? What is it proud of you for? How have you been taking good care of it?

If your emotions felt safe enough to spill over, how would it feel to let them flow? Can you let them be raw emotions without adding labels to them? Do you feel safe enough to be "emotional," however that looks?

If the universe inside of you wrote you a letter, what would it say? This is a profoundly healing process. Sit down in a quiet moment and let your pen flow onto paper without overthinking the words. Let the words be positive (otherwise it's your ego in disguise).

If you could do one thing today to align with bliss, what would you do? How do your dreams wish to be actualized?

ANCHOR INTO YOUR HEARTSPACE

Your Soul, although formless and unbound, can be accessed through your heartspace. Dropping into your heartspace has two magical effects. First, it brings you down and out of your mind's chatter, away from the noise and into a space of quiet knowing. Second, it calms the whole body as you're stimulating the vagus nerve. It's a tangible, loving touchpoint that connects you to the cosmos and light within.

Here's a way to open your heart to the wisdom of your Soul. Press your hands together in prayer position. Gently push your thumbs into the middle of your chest. Take a deep breath and tune in to the heart-opening sensation. Let bliss flow from your Soul through your whole being. Sit with this feeling for as long as you want. Keep breathing deeply. Welcome home.

Whenever you have a question for your Highest Self, simply place your hands on your heart center (in prayer position or any way that feels comfortable), take a deep breath, and trust that the answer will come.

LIVING THROUGH YOUR PHYSICAL SENSES

Living in communion with yourself comes to life when you engage fully with your physical senses. Your senses are always turned on, even when you meditate or sleep. No matter how distracted you are, your senses do not ever stop interacting intimately with the world around you and informing you of what you need to know.

Earlier in this book, I mentioned the endless stream of sensory information that floods your senses and how this informs your intuition. Now, I'd like to expand on that and provide you with an inspired way to live sensually.

Living sensually involves being consciously aware of and connected to life. It's a way to mindfully embrace your environment and let your sensations guide and gratify you. When you live sensually in every moment, you'll find bliss is only a wink away.

Where attention goes, energy flows. You won't notice how this book feels in your hands until you connect to your hands and the texture of each page. You won't tune in to what the pages sound like when they turn until you open your ears to them. As you are so focused on reading with your eyes, your capacity for tuning in to other senses is limited while you are engaged visually with the words and their meanings. That's completely natural; it's how you're supposed to function. Generally, you won't tune in to your senses until you *need to*—like if you cut your finger on a page or drop this book on your toe—or until you *choose to*. Choosing to connect to your senses brings your intuitive sensations to life.

Your nose is possibly the most undervalued of all the physical senses. But your sense of smell has such a strong connection to emotions that its value is immense. The smells and fragrances around you will only be noticeable when you tune in to them— that is, when you stop to smell the posies, your coffee, or your lover—or when they are strong enough to get your attention—like the smoke from burning toast or an overwhelming fragrance.

Your mouth constantly tastes, even when it's empty. And if you've ever eaten a meal while completely distracted by screens, you may have noticed that you hardly tasted a thing. That's why mindful eating is so important, not only for ultimate enjoyment, but also for your body to recognize what and when you are eating so it's able to prime your digestion. Some flavors will stand out more than others, either because they're scrumptious or they're spoiled. Connecting to food is a beautiful and nourishing way to gently move your self-awareness to the significant nutritional aspect of your life.

Your ears are awake in every moment. Sensitive people will notice that too much noise—even everyday noise like radio or traffic—may feel overwhelming. Personally, I enjoy relaxing music without advertisements, no radio, very little TV, and lots of noise from nature, musical instruments, and my kids. I'm conscious of what I listen to and how it makes me feel, so, as much as possible, I will set up my environment to be calming, nurturing, and gentle on the ears.

Your hands are especially good at taking in the world around you through the sense of touch, but you may not notice that the silky skin of your whole body is switched on and informing you all day and night. You'll feel discomfort if your socks are too tight, if the weather or air-conditioning is too hot or cold, and a thousand other pieces of information every minute of the day. Often, it's not until you have a bath, swim, massage, or sex that you feel sensual all over, but you can give yourself this feeling whenever you desire with a self-massage or a barefoot walk in nature using your hands to experience the wild world around you.

Your eyes lead the way through the world. It's with your miraculous sight that you marvel at, navigate through, and understand your surroundings. Your eyes are one of the key sources of information for your intuition; they provide an endless stream of awareness while you're awake. Tuning in to your eyesight consciously and with wonder, without the need to form an opinion on all you see, will bring you so much mindful joy and connection to the present moment.

With your senses, you can intentionally discover and profoundly appreciate yourself and your extraordinary world a whole lot deeper.

CONSCIOUS AND CREATIVE EATING

Connecting with food and your body with humble appreciation and awe will fertilize the soil from which self-awareness grows. When you feed your body what it needs, you're giving yourself the greatest fuel for a conscious life. Without good food, it's a struggle to connect to and love your body and the lifeforce that emanates from it, because your energy relies on the food you eat so intimately.

My plate is far from clean—my insatiable chocolate cravings can attest to that—but I'm intuitive about what I eat and drink. I'm aware when I'm eating something to satisfy an emotion rather than a real physical craving, and usually I'm in tune and in love with all I devour. Thanks to my intuitive Mama, who is an incredible cook and shame-free eater, I grew up with a grounded and healthy attitude toward food and never saw any reason to diet. To this day, I carry with me an open mind around food, and I love experimenting with all I see, so long as my body is interested.

The science of dieting is quite shocking. Steven Hawks, a professor of health science, conducted a study looking at the eating habits of college students. He compared naturally intuitive eaters with those who were not intuitive and looked at their overall health. This was his conclusion: "What makes intuitive eating different from a diet is that all diets work against human biology, whereas intuitive eating teaches people to work with their own biology, to work with their bodies, to understand their bodies … it's really about increasing awareness and understanding of your body. It's a nurturing approach to nutrition, health, and fitness as opposed to a regulated, coercive, restrictive approach. That's why diets fail, and that's why intuitive eating has a better chance of being successful in the long term."[8]

I've never been on a diet in my life. I've tried different approaches to eating, as well as a few wayward cleanses, but I simply will not restrict my intake of the foods I love. If a healer suggests I cut out an ingredient or food group, I do so *if* it feels right. If a particular supplement, herb, ingredient, or approach is recommended, I'll take it on as long as my body approves wholeheartedly.

Intuitive guidance, a fluid approach, connection to self, and large doses of love are all necessary to nourishing yourself because your body is changing in every moment. Nobody knows your body better than you do, and the food you eat doesn't define who you are. Food doesn't make you spiritual or intuitive. Vegans are no more intuitive than meat-eaters. Raw foodies are no more spiritual than those who eat cooked food. There's no "perfect" way to eat that makes you more mystical. Being conscious about your food and knowing what's in it, where it came from, and how the ingredients have been treated and grown are more important for your body than following someone else's ideas of "right" or "wrong" foods. Your body needs what your body needs. And intuitively, it will always truly crave healthy food.

Be curious, ask for advice, get inspired, but let your clever body have the last word. If you take your time connecting within, you'll

8. Hawks, Madanat, Hawks, and Harris, "The Relationship between Intuitive Eating and Health Indicators among College Women," 331–336.

be familiar with the messages you're receiving from your wise body.

Food is sustenance. Food is nourishment, vitality, and health. Food is fun, connection, and bliss. Food contributes enormously to your energy, vibes, sleep, emotions, thoughts, and pretty much everything else. Some people have more resilient constitutions, while others are sensitive to every little bite. Embrace who you are and how your gut works.

Deep down, you know when an ingredient is nourishing you or not. Your intuition will tell you when a craving is coming from your body or your ego. Here's a clue: if you feel attached to the craving, like you desperately need it, then it's your ego talking. It's from fear. If you feel like it would be enjoyable, but you're not obsessed, then it's your body. It's from love. And when you pause and connect inward to your loving and honest heart, you will know when and what to eat.

This may be confusing at first if you've never aligned with your body's nutritional needs. If you struggle to understand how food makes you feel, then I would recommend you keep a food journal. Write down everything you eat and how it makes you feel. Don't count calories or kilojoules. Leave guilt and shame out of the book (and your life). Simply begin to notice what food is genuinely nourishing you with good energy and what food isn't aligned with your body. How do you feel twenty minutes after you eat? How did you sleep at night? How easily did you wake in the morning? How was your mood affected? This will change over time and be affected by your lifestyle, too, so don't be rigid or fastidious about it; just gently allow your consciousness around food to unfold.

Keeping a mindful food journal is about becoming joyfully aware of food and nourishment. How do you know what food is beneficial for your whole, beautiful being? It feels good. *It feels really damn good all over.*

If you want to feel good more often, learn to love organic and local whole foods like eggs, line-caught local fish, grass-fed meat, seasonal fruit and vegetables, nuts and seeds, and high-quality olive and coconut oils … if your body can handle them. This is a great place to start. Add a dash of herbs and a heap of love, and you'll be satisfied all the way to your Soul.

Get creative. Find recipes that revolve around these wholesome, basic, nutritious foods. Keep exploring and experimenting. Keep eating your favorite sweets, treats, and snacks as well—just look for ways to make them yourself with whole ingredients or buy healthy versions.

Support your local farmers, grow your own herbs and vegetables, and find ways to source your food from people who look after Mother Earth. When your food is closely connected to the earth's energy and rhythm, you'll feel this pulsing through your body after each mouthful.

Reach out for help when you need it. When you just can't give up chocolate or ice cream, when you struggle to stick to a healthy meal plan, when confusion reigns supreme in the kitchen, or when you don't know how to cook, then find a psychologist, nutritionist, or food coach who can shine a little light on your situation.

When you are anchored in love, food will be a pleasure to eat, it will make you feel good, you'll eat only when you're hungry, and you'll stop when you're almost full.

If you're about to eat something and you're either not hungry or not conscious of what you're doing, pause for a moment and ask yourself: What was I just thinking? What emotion am I numbing with this food? What does my intuition want me to know? Be gentle with yourself, yet deeply curious. The honest answers to those questions may help you unravel any unhealthy emotional eating issues.

Trust and accept yourself. Connect with your body's signals. Use your hands. Make a mess. Lick the bowl. Food is one of the greatest pleasures of life. And I promise you this: when you eat a delicious, wholesome, varied, exciting, plant-based diet, your intuition will have the best chance of thriving.

Rediscover Yourself in Nature

Nature is an extension of the wild worlds within you, and you are a valuable part of nature's mystery and wilderness. Nature's cycles, moods, and elements affect us all, just as nature is affected profoundly by humanity. The earth, atmosphere, moon, sun, four elements, stars, other planets, and all the interactions and movements around and within our solar system have an impact on how we feel, think, and act.

Connecting with nature—going outdoors, soaking in the morning sun, watching the moon, conducting ceremonies to invoke the elements, understanding astrology, being with animals, healing with crystals, using herbal medicine—will allow you to tune in to your body so much deeper. It will foster a wholehearted consciousness of the universe within. By connecting with nature, we're intuitively connecting with—and healing—our own wild, natural spirit.

Great Spirit is in you and me and the winds between, in every insect and animal, every tree and rock, all the streams and rivers, the wide oceans and the continents, too. Great Spirit is in the fire and the layers of the earth, in the seen and unseen. When you're in nature, you're in the arms of Great Spirit.

Mother Earth is one of the greatest intuitive guides you'll ever find. She's a force to be loved and honored. She can ground your energy, bring you out of your headspace and into your heart, into your body, into your energy, and into your eternal Soul. Spend time in nature. Search through the endlessly wondrous creations, for they mirror and echo the parts of you that you're longing to find.

Let nature inspire your healing. Let the trees, the timekeepers, share their knowledge. Let the rocks, the recordkeepers, hold space for you to find your ancient, still voice. Let the flowers reflect your own divine beauty. Let the animals energetically provide you with their medicine. Let the elements reset your inner compass. Let the storms cleanse you whole. Let the sunshine fill your being. Let the stars guide you home.

Get grounded. Put your bare feet on Mother Earth. If you can't get outside, then visualize nature; your brain won't know the difference. I've written the following meditation to help you connect deeply to nature on the days when you can't venture outside.

· RITUAL ·
Mother Earth Visualization

Sit comfortably where you won't be disturbed. Slowly and effortlessly close your eyes and breathe deeply into your belly and lungs with precious air from the trees. Let it all out with a relaxing sigh. Imagine you're sitting on a wide, warm rock with your feet on the dirt and trees all around you, tall, strong, and vital. Visualize roots sprouting out of your feet, moving through the earth all the way to the core as you energetically allow Mother Earth to restore your health with waves of healing energy. Allow this to continue for as long as you require. If you need to, send your physical and emotional stress into the earth for nature to transmute into love. Take note of any messages you receive. You may visualize animals, flowers, or other beings in nature. Take your time with this intuitive process. Give thanks and, when you're ready, gently open your eyes.

When you ground yourself regularly, you'll come to appreciate more peace, higher energy, lighter emotions, and a clearer mind. This allows intuitive messages to come through much clearer and more regularly. Life will flow, just as the cycles of nature flow.

Connecting to nature and grounding yourself is such a powerful and necessary practice as you grow spiritually. The more you meditate and connect with your Highest Self and the higher realms, the more you need to ground your body into the earth.

Enlightenment needs embodiment. Wide-open insight needs deep-rooted instinct. As above, so below. Keep connecting to the natural, incredible world within and all around you. It's all from the same great mystery, guiding us in the watery depths of our eternal being.

EMBRACING SENSITIVITIES

Sensitivities are such a valuable part of being human. To taste the full flavor of a ripe strawberry. To marvel with your whole being at a sunrise. To lose your mind in a kiss. To embrace all your wild emotions. To feel Mother Earth's heart beating with yours. To weep and cheer for the characters in a play, movie, or book. To empathetically understand people on a deep level. To hear music with every cell of your being.

These are gifts. Treasure them.

I have completely and undoubtedly always been a highly sensitive creature. Just ask my Mama. Ever since I was a baby, I was sensitive to *all* things. I've also always been self-aware. It's only in the last ten years that I've realized these two valuable assets are intricately linked at the heart.

As a young adult, I cried more than most people, I was scared easily, and I felt what others were going through in such a palpable way. When I moved in with my boyfriend (who is now my husband), I remember feeling so overwhelmed on one particularly difficult day. I felt like I couldn't switch my senses off; they felt so raw and bare.

On this intense day, I felt like falling apart. I cried to my man, saying, "I'm so sensitive I can't stand it. I just want to be normal!" And he said something I'll never forget: "Honey, I know you're sensitive to the upsetting things, but you're also sensitive to the beautiful things. Can't you see?" That was my first clear understanding of a highly sensitive person. To see life this way was a surprising gift I only started to unwrap with gratitude that day.

When I was in my early thirties, my husband and I started trying to conceive a baby. After three years and a few early miscarriages, we were referred to a naturopath for some much-needed support. This naturopath was critical to my spiritual evolution, because she taught me about the importance of cleaning out the toxins from my body and home.

We tossed out the chemicals and anything that wasn't natural and healthy from the cleaning cupboard, laundry, pantry, kitchen, bathroom, and everywhere else. We replaced them with the simplest and most natural products we could find. We ate healthy food. And we spent more time in nature than ever.

It felt like a rebirth. After four months of clean, delicious living, I fell pregnant with our beautiful son, Lucas. Ever since then, I have been gently conscious about what I put into and on my body. I'm not fastidious about being "clean," but I ensure that everything is as close to nature as possible.

Then my daughter, Ariella, was born, four and a half years after Lucas came smiling into this world, and my sensitivities became even more raw. While I was pregnant with and breastfeeding her, I was visiting a number of health professionals. In accordance with their advice, I moved away from the foods that were intolerable to her, namely seafood, eggs, nuts, dairy, wheat, gluten, and night-shades. When she turned one and I finished breastfeeding, I was able to eat anything I wanted again … finally, after all these years of preparing for birth, being pregnant, and breastfeeding, I had my body back.

But I was in such a deprived and depleted state that I didn't get the essential help I needed to nourish my body. Instead, I became a chocoholic and a stubborn eater of all the croissants. I also didn't realize that I'd internalized a profound sense of fear around the foods that I'd cut out when I was pregnant and breastfeeding, assuming they could potentially harm my baby. So instead of gaining strength and resilience, my sensitivities became worse. Over the years that followed, I fearfully gave up many other foods. I'd become edgy around food because I hadn't taken time to heal, or check in with my body, or love myself deeper.

I assumed it was the food that was causing my anxious symptoms, sleepless nights, and mood swings, when all along it was the fearful beliefs that were the basis of these symptoms.

Thanks to a few incredible healers and friends, I've recently experienced one of the healthiest mindsets around food that I've ever had. I intuitively eat a wide range of beautiful foods with renewed love, appreciation, and vigor. I sleep well, I exercise regularly, my focus is clear, and I'm able to live mindfully.

As you clear out the chemicals, people, habits, hobbies, food, and false ideas that are getting in the way of your intuitive abilities, you're allowing for a greater connection between your mind, body, Soul, and spirit, because your energy is flowing freely, your heart is open to the healing vibration of love, and your body is in a state of grace.

NATURAL LIVING INSPIRATION

Here are some ways you can gradually tend to your immediate and expanded environment. Start with them all or choose one to begin with and see how the ripple effect feels in your life. Intuitively try your own ideas as well that focus on nature and living simply.

- Look after your garden with only natural sprays.
- Love your skin and choose only completely natural beauty, body, and bath products.
- Clear out any food from your fridge or pantry that contains unhealthy ingredients.
- Filter your water and ditch plastic containers, bottles, and wraps from your kitchen.
- Stick with ceramic, wood, bamboo, stainless steel, and glass.
- Stock only natural cleaners in your laundry or make your own.
- Wear clothing made from natural fibers.
- Support your local creative communities and buy furniture, toys, and homewares made from nature's finest.
- Before you buy anything new, see if you can purchase it secondhand instead.
- Watch less television, look at your phone less, and never leave a screen on if you're not watching it.
- Open your windows as much as you can to let nature cleanse your abode.
- Invite only people who make you feel good into your home.
- Clean and bless your car regularly.

Dancing with Creativity

Creativity is how you bring your ideas and dreams to life; it's the way you access and express your sacred inner spirit. It's a physical, mental, emotional, and deeply spiritual way of connecting within to the depths of your being and articulating or manifesting something inspired in the world. Creative connection is precious and a potent way to discover more about you.

Your own unique style of creativity will be different from everyone else's. Don't think for a second that it's all been done before or nothing is original anymore. *You are original.* What you create doesn't have to be practical, sellable, shareable, tangible, or easily understood. It doesn't need to be complicated, perfect, or expected. Just authentic.

Creativity is only ever asking you to make time to be fully expressed. You don't need to commit to only one creative outlet; you have permission to be a free and easy creative hustler. You might want to express your imagination through painting, sculpture, drawing, design, photography, fashion, felting, knitting, crocheting, singing, music, dancing, writing, editing, gardening, or cooking. And you definitely do not need to take lessons—unless you want to—or be professionally trained to explore your chosen craft.

Sing in the car. Write wholeheartedly. Make crochet gifts for friends. Play in the garden. Dance on your balcony. Paint with your fingers. Do it your way. Let your dreams and desires bring your gifts to life in any way that delights you. Let this connection between your mind and your wholehearted talents inspire your life and lead you gently, leisurely, and with immense pleasure along your creative purpose.

Go in with a full and daring heart. You cannot lose or fail. In creativity, you can do no wrong. Let your purpose be your fully expressed life—not a particular job or endpoint, but your daily dipping and diving into creative bliss. Let your intuition guide you toward what lights you up, because what lights you up is guiding you onward, like stars illuminating the sacred path before you.

The more you indulge in your creative nature and the more you express your ancient talents, the more you are loosening up the rational mind. When you loosen up your logic, you find creative solutions to problems, you see life as a cascade of opportunity, and you inevitably tap into your inner flow. And you find *immeasurable joy*.

· PRACTICE ·
Wild Energy Soul Prompts

Get really, bravely creative with your heart in these questions. Sit somewhere peaceful, light a candle, take a few deep breaths, and begin. Be patient with yourself. Sometimes you need to ask yourself the same question a few times before you get to the gold that lies beneath.

There are no right or wrong answers, there is no deadline, and you don't need to do anything with this outpouring of ink. This practice is a simple way to get to understand, love, and accept yourself. No judgment; just let it all flow.

Let's start with a look at what lowers your energy:

- What makes you feel frazzled or scattered?
- What or who drains your energy, leaving you feeling low, exhausted, or anxious?
- Who or what makes you feel disconnected from love, yourself, joy, or purpose?

- What blocks your creativity? What thoughts, stories, and fears have you created around this?
- What are you willing to change ... and how?

Now let's look at what raises your vibration:

- What makes you feel serene and peaceful, and what lights you up?
- Who or what makes you feel connected to yourself, Spirit, nature, or love?
- Who or what makes you feel at home, at ease, and happy?
- What brings you closer to your creative heart?
- What's your favorite thing about you? What do others say about you that feels really good?

CONNECT WITH THE COSMOS

Now that you're more intimately connected with your richly sacred and creative inner world, let's look around you at the presence of Spirit and how it is impacting and guiding you every day.

GUIDANCE FROM SPIRIT

Along my spiritual journey, I've met many powerfully supportive and loving beings that are mostly invisible to my human eyes. These members of my Divine Team—the collective of light beings who work closely with me—are an imperative part of my life as an earthling. They are my ancestors, my tribe, my masters, my friends, and my angels. I adore them. Spirit—meaning all beings of light in energetic form—is slightly different from "spirit," which means the sacred energy that moves through our being.

Perhaps you're ready to connect to Spirit in a whole new way, or maybe you're looking to deepen your connection to the Divine Team that has been sent just for you. Maybe you're curious to know who's out there before you take the next step. Wherever you are and whatever you desire is perfect.

You don't need a solid understanding of your team to have a strong intuition or to receive insight. You only need to connect to the love within. But in my experience, an awareness of *and* a trusting relationship with Spirit will strengthen the light that flows through you as it guides you in divinely aligned ways.

When you receive new information or a fresh perspective from Spirit, it comes through your crown as pure *insight*. The way you understand and integrate this wisdom is through your *intuition*. Knowing which energies or information is not for you comes through your *instinct*. All three of your inner guides are strengthened when you tune in to Spirit.

Here's something I know for sure about cosmic Spirit: there's an unlimited amount of strength, guidance, healing, and love just waiting for you to tap into it.

Let's look at the beings who live in Spirit and how they can help.

SPIRIT GUIDES

I connect with my team of Spirit Guides daily; whether it's a general gratitude shout-out, a meditation to connect, a prayer, messages through oracle cards, or an easy conversation on the go, I regularly call them in for gatherings and imagine them sitting all around me. I love my squad. They change occasionally as I grow spiritually, but I know I always have the right guides at the right time in my group.

When I connect to them, I ask for miracles, healing, business advice, parenting tips, peace, bliss, direction, love, or anything my heart desires to feel or know. I send them love, gratitude, offerings, and joyful thoughts. There are many ways to connect, as you'll see below, and your spirit will feel nourished every time you do.

We all have a stellar bunch of guides with us in each lifetime; we choose each other before we incarnate. Some Spirit Guides knew us in a past life, others are Ascended Masters like Jesus, Mary Magdalene, Buddha, or Quan Yin. Your main Spirit Guide is with you for life (and many lives besides). Each guide comes with a particular purpose, a specific kind of light (information) that they impart into your field of consciousness. They want to guide you to live your best life possible according to your Highest Self and your Soul's purpose.

All Spirit Guides and Ascended Masters used to live as humans before they became enlightened, which means they don't need to incarnate again. Even though they're enlightened, they still understand our humanness in all its shades of light and dark: joy, love, sex, food, pleasure, nature, pain, anger, shame, and everything else about being human. They get it. So, you can vent and scream and cry and rage or love and sing and dance and play, and they're with you through it all, holding space for your expression and growth with endless empathy and compassion.

To connect with your team, simply set an intention and open your heart. Trust that you have guides all around you at all times wanting to love, guide, and protect you—if you are open to this and ask for it, it will happen. Trust that you are safe with them. Trust that miracles are a natural way of life when you are in tune with the highest guidance.

Once you've established a connection with your guides, you'll notice their signs and guidance more regularly. Personally, I see feathers, butterflies, symbols, and signs on a daily basis, and I feel goose bumps and shivers when they are telling me I'm on the right track. I notice flickering lights, too—not actual lights that flicker, but near-invisible dancing orbs of my guides, fairies, angels, and other light beings.

Life is never dull when you're connected to your Divine Team.

· RITUAL ·
Spirit Guide Connection Meditation

Here's a meditation to connect you directly with a Spirit Guide. Hold an intention—perhaps you want to meet a particular guide or find an answer—and let go of expectations. Sit comfortably with your feet flat on the floor and palms turned upward.

Gently slow down your breathing. Breathe in through your nose, filling your belly and expanding your lungs. Gently breathe out of your mouth. Feel your connection to the core of Mother Earth through your feet. Call in Great Spirit to protect you from all but love and light from the highest dimensions. Open your crown chakra to establish a connection to the Divine. Keep breathing slowly.

Now ask your main Spirit Guide to come close to you. Relax. Trust this process. Soon you'll feel their gently loving presence. If their presence isn't obvious, keep asking them to come closer until their presence is clear. Notice how you feel when they're close and where they are located in the field around you.

Take time to soak up their love. Go with whatever vision or feelings you are sent. Ask them for their name or a sign or a message. Trust what you feel, hear, and/or see. The first words that come to you are your message; the first vision you see is your sign. Take your time with them until you feel your connection is complete—this may take a few minutes or a while longer. When you are ready, thank them. Close your energy field by imagining a cloud of healing light around you. Feel back into your body and open your eyes.

When you are finished with your meditation, you may want to take notes or get creative and draw or paint. Savor the feeling.

ARCHANGELS

The Archangels have carried me through many dark times. They've brought light to my toughest days, raised my spirit when I felt consumed by my depths, and shown me miracle after astounding miracle. On the good days they've been just as close, celebrating my achievements (through rainbows and all sorts of beauty), leaving me love notes (in songs and books), helping me heal myself or clients (through various insights), and showing me how to develop my gifts (in meditations, books, signs, and symbols).

I laugh with them. I talk out loud to them often. I readily connect with them when I'm out for a walk. I see orbs of light when I'm relaxed and they're close. I see rays of colored lights when I know they're traveling with me. They're my friends, my brothers and sisters, messengers of Great Spirit, and sacred and supernatural beings who are available to everyone all the time.

They're our celestial companions, deliverers of light and peace. Archangels have never incarnated as a human or any other being on another planet. They live in a higher realm. Although we're all made from the same love and light, Archangels fly quite close to the Source.

Occasionally I'll hear their name when they're nearby. Sometimes I'll see them in a dream or meditation. Other times I'll keep meeting people with the same or similar name to an angel. It's all very intuitive, but the more I trust my inner knowing, the easier it is to know why they're near.

The first angel I connected with was Archangel Michael. He's my protector, my brother, my right-hand angel. I see his blue orbs most days, reminding me of his presence, protection, and love. He reminds me of the power within me. I simply, humbly, and profoundly cherish him. Once I saw him so extraordinarily large and close, there was no doubt of his presence and message. It was the day before I flew to California in 2017, and I was feeling nervous. Flying doesn't usually make me nervous, but temporarily leaving my family and a life I adored left my tummy feeling ruffled. As I was driving to a friend's house the night before my flight, I saw a long, bright blue, enormous light flying alongside my car. I was in a tunnel, so the light was completely dazzling and about three times as long as my car. In my heart, I knew it was Archangel Michael, assuring me that I would be protected the entire time. The relief in my mind and body was so welcomed.

The next Archangel I connected with was Gabriel. In 2011, I had a dream that I was at a farmer's market when I saw a woman called Gabrielle, one of my favorite singers from the nineties. (I didn't realize in the dream that it was an angel visiting me; I was just excited to hear beautiful music from a singer I loved.) She said that if we all stayed and listened to her latest song, we'd win a prize. So, I stayed, enjoyed the sweet tune, and afterward she handed me a pair of huge, feathery wings as my reward. I put them on and went to find my husband and some organic fruit. I thought it was a cute dream, but it wasn't until I woke up and was telling my husband about the dream that I suddenly exclaimed, "Oh my heart honey, Archangel Gabriel just gave me wings!"

The following day I was in a bookstore when a book on Archangel Gabriel fell into my hands. I didn't know why I was in the shop—there was barely a spiritual book in sight and no other books on angels. I stood there with this heavenly book in my hands, wondering in awe at how quickly and easily the angels work. I read the book in a few days and couldn't believe how perfect this beautiful angel was for me. Gabriel works with mothers and writers most of all, and ever since then, her presence has always brought me insight and reassurance.

Some of the angels I'm still getting to know, so don't rush or think you have to connect to all of them at once. Take your time. Notice their signs. I look for butterflies—real or in drawings, art, social media, clothes, or anywhere else they might appear. For me, the color of the butterfly relates to the color of the angel.

Each of the seven main Archangels has their own color and their own qualities and responsibilities:

Archangel Michael. Blue. Protection, guidance, and strength. Helps with safety, direction, self-esteem, motivation, courage, commitment, faith, energy, vitality, life purpose, and releasing fear.

Archangel Gabriel. White/deep gold. Parenting and communication. Helps those working as writers or anywhere in the media; assists with fertility, pregnancy, and parenting (especially mothering). Insight, communication, awareness, truth, and strength. Full expression.

Archangel Raphael. Emerald green. Healer of physical, emotional, mental, and spiritual bodies. Assists with complete health, well-being, and wholeness. Helps reduce or eliminate addictions or cravings, supports and guides healers, and helps find lost pets.

Archangel Uriel. Ruby red/purple. Insight, clarity, peace. Inspires visions, problem-solving, writing, new ideas, studying, and tests.

Soothes conflict and replaces it with peace, clarity, and insight. Helps release mental and emotional patterns that are anchored in fear. Encourages deep trust.

Archangel Chamuel. Pink. Unconditional love and adoration. Helps with career, life purpose, finding lost items, building and strengthening relationships, and world peace. Releases resentment, fear, and pain.

Archangel Zadkiel. Violet. Forgiveness, mercy, and benevolence. Helps with emotional healing, compassion, freedom, and memory. Releases pain, bitterness, and negativity.

Archangel Jophiel. Golden yellow. Creativity, beauty, and art. Helps to manifest beauty; supports artists, awakening, self-awareness, inspiration, hope, and joy. Releases prejudice and ignorance.

· RITUAL ·
Angel Connection Meditation

This meditation is to connect you with an Archangel. I encourage you to hold an intention to meet a particular Archangel but leave expectations behind. Sit comfortably with your feet flat on the floor and your palms turned upward.

Slow your breathing to a comfortable, resting rhythm. Feel your connection to the core of the earth through your feet. Open the top of your energy field above your head to establish a connection with the Divine. Keep breathing slowly.

Now ask for the Archangels to come close. Choose an angel that you would like to work with or stay open to whoever is meant to meet with you today. Soon you'll feel their unique and loving presence, and you may also see their color. Notice how you feel when they're close. Talk to them in your mind as though they were sitting with you, and trust what you hear in response. The first words that come to you are your message. Take your time. When you feel complete, give thanks. Feel back into your body and open your eyes.

Enjoy the connection. It doesn't matter where you're at with spirituality or religion; angels are not bound or restricted by beliefs, time, or space. Speak to them wherever you go to strengthen the connection. Delight in their presence when you call on them. Ask to see butterflies to support your decisions.

When you're finished with your meditation, you may want to take notes or get creative and draw or paint.

Loved Ones

You have Loved Ones around you right now as you're reading this. Loved Ones in spirit who have left the human form you once knew and taken flight on wings of their eternal Soul to their spirit home.

Not all of your departed Loved Ones are close to you, simply because they're not all meant to be your helpers, but the ones that are, are available to help you if you ask. These ancestral Spirit Guides know your life and its challenges well, and they can bring you great comfort, wisdom, and hope anytime you need them. Plus, they empathize with your ancestral lineage, so they can guide you toward deeper healing for you and past and future generations.

Personally, I'm connected to many women on my matriarchal side. This particular lineage has come through strongly many times in personal meditation, journaling, and psychic readings. My Grandma (Mama's Mama) and I are very close, even though we didn't have much of a relationship earthside. Our family didn't live close to her, so I didn't know her as a child. She didn't have an easy life, so she's passionate about helping me heal our lineage so that our future generations and I will experience life more easily and aligned with our true nature.

Loved Ones will connect with you by being present and available. You'll know when they're close because you will

- think of them often or spontaneously;
- keep an object of theirs close to you;
- smell their perfume or favorite flower;
- hear a song that reminds you of them;
- feel their presence; or
- meet people repeatedly with the same name as them.

Loved Ones in spirit will usually send signs to show you that they're close. They will help you grow into the best version of yourself in many different ways. They will inspire you to be genuinely happy. They will show you the deepest way to heal. Their capacity to guide you from the world of Spirit is eternal and surprisingly specific, and it helps if you're a willing recipient of their love and wisdom. You can even reach out to them and make requests for help on earth. Nothing is too small for them to help you with. Having a daily meditation practice will give you an opportunity to connect with Loved Ones on a regular basis. If you can't hear them clearly, trust that they can hear you, and look for other ways that they may be communicating with you.

I would recommend seeing a psychic medium if you are unsure which Loved Ones are guiding you, if you have connected with a Loved One but felt uneasy, or if you need to know something specific about a Loved One but you're unable to receive the answer. Like all Spirit Guides, most Loved Ones are available for a chat anytime.

· RITUAL ·
Connection with Loved Ones Meditation

Connecting with Loved Ones, just like Archangels and Spirit Guides, can happen spontaneously throughout your day or consciously in a meditation. If there is a Loved One you wish to meet, hold a loving intention to meet them now. Sit comfortably with your feet flat on the floor and your palms turned upward.

Slow your breathing to a naturally calm rhythm. Feel how supported you are by Mother Earth and how loved you are by Spirit. Keep breathing slowly.

Imagine the Loved One whom you wish to connect with now. Call them in your mind by name, see their face, and ask them to come closer until you feel a change in the energy around you. You may feel their presence, hear their voice, receive a clear message, see them with or above you, or otherwise know they are near. Be patient and keep your mind clear. Trust in the process.

It may take time to get a clear idea of where they are and how they appear to you. Express your gratitude for their life and their enduring love and send them blessings.

Your Loved Ones in spirit have so much love and guidance for you, so if you weren't able to get a clear connection with them today, try another day or a different way. Write them a letter and let their answer flow through your pen. Talk to them as you walk through nature. Ask them to help you with specific problems (they relish being sent on earth missions). Encourage them to show you signs and symbols.

Whenever I connect to clients' Loved Ones in mediumship readings, I almost always feel a sense of pride and celebration. We are often so hard on ourselves, and our ancestors want us to see how wonderfully and courageously we have co-created our lives.

WISDOM OF SIGNS AND SYMBOLS

Signs and symbols are the potent, wordless love language of the universe. They are messages from Spirit that convey so much without a single word. Nothing could be simpler or more powerful. Signs and symbols are how we playfully engage with the intelligence and serendipity of the universe.

Synchronicities are "meaningful coincidences," according to Carl Jung. They can be sweetly subtle or strikingly obvious episodes of divine timing. The more open your mind and the deeper you trust your intuitive path, the more obvious the synchronicities.

Here's an everyday example of how these play out in my life: Butterflies are one of my favorite *symbols*. The meaning of this symbol is a *sign* from angels that I'm guided, loved, and on the right path. *Synchronicity* is seeing this symbol multiple times in one day and knowing that angels are near, supporting my course of action.

Symbols may come from Archangels, Ascended Masters, Spirit Guides, Loved Ones, Mother Nature, or your Highest Self. Sometimes it's a cosmic "coincidence" delivering goodness or guidance into your life. When you notice symbols that seem to have a personal reference, take a moment to ask yourself what it wants to tell you and where it came from. Meditate with it, journal through it, and practice opening your inner senses to discover what it means for you.

If you would like more information on the symbol, you can always look it up online or in a book to see what experts in the field have to say. I always recommend tuning in to the symbol directly first before you look it up. Your personal interpretation is the most important one; however, the online meaning can add another layer to your intuitive understanding of the symbol.

Here are some of the most common and meaningful signs and symbols and how to work with them.

Animals, Birds, and Insects

If you see an animal, bird, or insect (in real life or elsewhere) and feel it has a message, connect with it and ask what it wants to share with you. Repeatedly seeing the same animal usually means it wants to connect with you and share its energy / medicine or message.

As I'm writing this, the tiniest praying mantis is creeping onto my computer's hard drive. It turns its head and looks straight at me. I'm in sweet shock because I've never seen such a small, curious creature like this, with such a delicate presence. It calms me just to look at him. I ask what his message is for me, and this pops into my mind: "Even the smallest gesture can have a positive ripple effect." With a smile on my face, I look up the meaning of the praying mantis online. The spiritual symbolism of these little creatures is stillness and meditation, which is just what I need to hear, as I have been ignoring my daily meditation practice for a little while. With gratitude and gentleness, I scoop him up and take him outside.

You might find that you've been connected to a particular animal or group of animals throughout your life. Personally, I've always had symbols, drawings, and images of the big cats within and around me. As a child, I was obsessed with them; I wanted calendars and books full of them—I wanted smaller, softer versions of them to hug at night, and often I would dream of them. To this day, I smile whenever I see an image of a tiger. My heart skips a beat. Quite often I'll close my eyes and thank the tiger for her medicine, for her fervent courage and humbling grace throughout my entire life. In 2018, when I was deep in ancestral healing, I saw tigers every single day for about two months. I glimpsed them on T-shirts, bags, laptops, prams, bumper stickers, social media, shoes, magazines, and books. Her medicine was working deeply within me, and I was grateful for her presence.

Nature

There is endless wisdom, guidance, and healing in the trees and bushes, rocks and waterways, flowers and fields, sunrises and sunsets, and all the divine energies outside. Hugging a tree or sitting on a large rock will do more for your instinct, intuition, and insight than you might imagine; it might give you a feeling of safety, comfort, expansiveness, and a message that you need to hear. Flowers can brighten your day, leading to unexpected insight. A sunset can give you a fresh perspective on a situation. Saltwater might bring you into a heart-opening meditative state.

Recently, my Soul sister Jodie gave me the most stunning bouquet of bright pink lilies; they were vibrant and bold. They spoke to me every day and made me feel loved and connected. Flowers have a way of lighting up a room, and at the time, I felt that they were showing me how to be a true friend by showing up, loving, and connecting with another. I looked up their meaning and discovered that they mean humility and devotion, which sound like the perfect ingredients for a strong friendship to me.

I'm a lifelong fan of immeasurably large trees. My Dad used to look to big gum trees with such awe and reverence, and now I do the same, only these days I hug them until I cry and their messages have poured through me. Big trees have been strengthened by the wind and their roots are so deep and unapologetic. I soak up the energy of tall trees every chance I get.

Music

Songs are sent to guide us and shower us with feelings of rapture, relaxation, and revelation. Trust that your intuition will pique when a song is played for you from your Divine Team. You may notice extra attention in your being, goose bumps, a stimulated emotion, or an inner knowing.

Songs may be guidance from Loved Ones who have passed over, from Spirit Guides, or from other spiritual messengers. They may be songs to cheer you up, make you dance, calm your nerves, speak to a problem, or simply love your free-spirited heart.

Music is a potent and poetic messenger of wisdom. I like to listen to the playlists that Spotify creates for me based on my listening preferences. The more I play music on Spotify, the more playlists they create. In these "random" and intuitive music selections, I find the cosmos is able to connect into and speak to my life.

Books

If a book cover gives you tingles, if you keep hearing about it from various friends you admire, or if it looks like it wants to fall off a shelf in a shop, take a moment to connect with it and see if it feels aligned with your energy.

Books are a rich source of guidance and worth investing in or borrowing if they feel like they could help or inspire you ... or even just give you a much-needed laugh. With books, you are able to access new, insightful ideas that fill up the well of information in your subconscious, bringing fresh ingredients into your intuitive spring.

You don't have to agree with a book in its entirety to gain insight from it. And remember, if you ever start a book and it doesn't feel good, put it away for another time (or never).

Recently, I was at my local library when my heart pulled me down an aisle I hadn't been down before. I saw a book called *Bad Yogi*, by Alice Williams, and without thinking, I put it on the pile of kid's books to take home. I started reading it after dinner that night, and I was finished in less than a week. I hadn't laughed that hard while joyously reading a memoir before, nor had I ever learned so much about yoga—plus there was a heap of spiritual insight that delighted me. I was so richly rewarded for following my intuition that day.

Divine Timing

Trust with your whole being in divine timing, even if it's confusing or doesn't make sense. Trust that the timing in your life is perfect. Have patience with all people, situations, and the inherent but unseen rhythm and order. Divine timing isn't linear, perfect, or meant to unfold according to our expectations.

Divine timing is the cosmic, intuitive order to all things. It's why you bump into people right when they have a message for you—sometimes spoken, but often unsaid. It's the synchronicities throughout your day that light up your path. It's the opportunities that arise just as you are ready for them. It's the events that you can't explain, but your Soul knows their worth. It's also the delays, interruptions, uncertainty, and other roadblocks that are out of your control. These are *all* signs for you to wait and trust. Breathe, surrender, and connect to your faith during these times; don't rush or push your way through them.

Roadblocks are annoying, but they bear gifts and wisdom. Delayed flights, traffic detours, cancelled appointments, technology interruptions, career divergence, limited progress, and all kinds of inconveniences can be in accordance with perfect timing, even when they don't feel that way. Be patient. You may never know why something went "wrong," but have faith that it was meant to be.

The key with timing is surrender. Often when we're pushing for a certain outcome, we're blinded to what we really need by our desperation. When we release, relax, and let go of expectations, the universe has space to deliver what we need, precisely when we need it.

Symbols

Sacred, guiding symbols are another way the universe speaks to us without the need for words. Symbolism is endless. If you see stars, angels, infinity, crosses, hearts, shapes, yin and yang, or other symbols, ask yourself what they mean to you. Is there a sensation you feel when you see the symbol? Is there a word or phrase that pops into your head? Have you seen it in meditation? There is so much information online, but I encourage you to ask your intuition first.

A few years ago, in a spiritual class, I was guided in a meditation to receive a symbol from a Spirit Guide. As my Guide drew closer and closer, I could sense her presence, a sensation that has never left me and that I recognize clearly when I need it. During the meditation, she handed me a six-pointed star with a circle around it. It felt like magic, like a powerful connection between us. Afterward, I recognized it as the Star of David, but I knew this symbol went beyond religion; it meant something else, something bigger. After many months of watching it pop up in my life in an endless stream of serendipitous discoveries, I looked it up online. Called a *hexagram*, it's historically connected to many religions and has many meanings, but the one I connect with the most points to the union of heaven and earth. I still see the hexagram regularly, and it always points to magic: the magic of connection with Spirit, the magic of universal intelligence, and the magic of becoming conscious within a human body.

· PRACTICE ·
Serendipity Soul Prompts

Open up to a fresh page in your notebook as you take a look back over the last month. Write down anything meaningful that stood out for you, perhaps in a dream or somewhere along your travels. Take a moment to consider what meanings may be tucked into the signs and symbols in your life.

Have you noticed any animals or insects around you lately? What are they and what do you think they want to tell you? How do you feel when they're around? What animals or insects do you feel have been close to you your whole life? What is their medicine, the feeling they wish to impart on you?

Think back to the last time you spent an hour or a day in nature. How did nature speak to your heart? How are you being called to spend more time in the wild outdoors? Where do you love to be, and what do you love to do in nature?

What songs have caused you to pause and take notice? What did the lyrics mean to you? Who do you think they were from?

When was the last time a book felt so wonderfully insightful? What was the name of the book and the main message you took from it? What book—or type of book—are you longing to read?

Have you noticed serendipity in your life lately? What coincidences or lucky chance encounters have you experienced? What do you believe causes life to be more or less fortuitous?

What are your favorite symbols? Where have you seen them? What do they mean to you?

Inner Sensing

Everyone has their own way of receiving guidance through psychic gifts that their Soul has been developing for lifetimes. *Intuitive* knowing is using your five *outer* senses (among other guidance) to live a life of self-awareness and alignment. *Psychic* knowing is tuning in to your *inner* senses (among other guidance) to receive insight.

Your sixth sense (sixth chakra / third eye) is essentially your portal to insight (seventh chakra / crown), the fresh ideas that flow from Spirit. These ideas and messages come through your inner senses, which, just like your outer senses, can be nourished and consciously connected to deeply.

The process by which you receive insight will be different from everyone else. You might know things with certainty and see visions occasionally, or you might hear words and be able to channel messages clearly, or you might feel sensations in your body and be able to smell scents from Spirit. You will have a strong primary inner sense and other senses that help you access information.

We can't always choose to receive insight in a specific way, just like we can't always choose our talents; we need to simply allow guidance to come through however it can. Surrender and connect; your Soul knows what to do if you can get your overthinking logical mind out of the way. An important point to make is that, in Spirit, things may seem irrational or nonsensical because information exists without the limitations of linear time and space. Don't try to make perfect sense of everything you receive.

My strongest sense is inner vision, or clairvoyance, but I also receive insight from other senses. I regularly hear messages whispered to me, smell scents wafting about when I'm home (it's usually my Grandpa's cologne), and have particularly strong knowings (psychic knowings are often confused with intuition, but if it's new information, it's always insight, not intuition).

My gifts are a mixed bunch that I could never have predicted, but they work powerfully together when I'm tuned in. Often the visions I see and the messages I hear are extremely faint, but with faith, focus, and gratitude, they get stronger. I encourage my clients who are strengthening their own inner senses not to expect bright, loud, or intense psychic insight. It would totally bowl them over. Welcome the subtle intelligence with gratitude. Refer back to the descriptions of the psychic gifts (on page 41) for a reminder of how they work within your being.

· RITUAL ·
Discover Your Psychic Gifts Meditation

Sit in a quiet place where you won't be disturbed. Ideally this meditation would take place standing up as it involves receiving insights, so if you have a way of doing this standing in peace, then do so. Otherwise, sit with your back naturally tall and straight and close your eyes.

Set an intention to receive psychic communication from the highest realms. Take a few deep breaths in through your nose and let the air flow fully out of your mouth.

When you're relaxed, open your inner senses. Use your imagination to bring them to life through an inner awakening. Notice your third eye, which may feel like a subtle buzz between your eyebrows. Sense your inner nose and allow it to smell pleasant or neutral fragrances from higher dimensions. Open your inner palate to experience flavors not of this earth. Let your ears turn inward and connect with Spirit. Imagine your body can feel all inner sensations and more. Now take a moment to ask Spirit to share a message with you using your strongest gift. Keep breathing and relax; trust that the information will come through.

You may see a faint vision. You may hear a whisper or see words tumble into your mind. You may receive the gift of a knowing or feel a particular sensation within your body. You may smell or taste something that has no obvious earthly source. Or you may feel a particular emotion. Try not to analyze it; simply let it come to you and unfold as it needs to.

If the message is too subtle, ask Spirit to come closer, to show you with complete clarity the message that is for you. Keep asking with a calm and trusting heart that you will receive what is meant for you. When you have received guidance, ask Spirit to take away any sensations that are not yours. Give thanks and gently open your eyes.

In the end, whether you received something radiant and clear, whisper thin, or nothing at all, always give thanks. Spirit was with you. The insight may unfold more clearly over the coming days— some people experience their insight more readily while actively living rather than while still in meditation. You have gifts, of this I'm sure, so believe in yourself, trust in Spirit, and be patient. Play with this connection as you move through your day. It may take time to tune in to an inner sense with certainty. If you do not feel like you are connecting to your gifts after a while, connect with a spiritual mentor who can guide you confidently.

INTUITIVE ORACLE INSIGHT

Every time I sit down with a set of oracle or tarot cards, I feel the wind stir around me. I know I'm entering a sacred realm. No reading is without a meaningful intention set with a grateful and respectful heart. I'm not just peering at shiny, pretty cards; I'm moving between worlds. I feel a door open to the higher realms as images, whispers, guidance, and knowing flood into my being. There's something so comforting and empowering about each reading.

Cards can be chosen according to any question, need, or desire that feels aligned in your heart. Choose one in the morning before you start your day, two at night to wrap up your thoughts and energy, a few on sacred occasions like new and full moons, larger spreads at the change of season, and juicy readings on your birthday and at the beginning of the year. Or do it your way. It's completely up to you.

Hundreds, perhaps thousands, of oracle card decks have been created across the globe over many centuries. You can find a set of cards for just about anything you can think of: Spirit, energy, intuition, angels, faeries, witches, Ascended Masters, animals, nature, ancient wisdom, crystals, affirmations, and decks for kids.

I used to be cautious about reading my own cards. I thought they were only for "deeply spiritual" people who were connected to Source and knew lots of spiritual stuff that I didn't have a clue about. I didn't buy them, even though I craved them for years. Finally, about ten years ago, I discovered a friend who was similar to me in her spiritual understanding, and yet she had a whole lot of oracle cards she played with all the time. I wanted in.

That's when I bought my first two decks. I used them every week, always in the same formula. As I shuffled them, I would consider a problem that I wanted help with. The first card represented the past, the second card spoke to the present, and the third card was all about the near future, not so much predicting the future but pointing to the next step for me to take.

I was deeply in awe and amazed by the insight that arose from each reading. Eventually, I bought a tarot deck. Inside the guidebook were so many different suggestions for how to lay out the cards—my mind and heart were suddenly ravenous, and I felt like I had reached a new level of cosmic co-creation.

For years I searched online for different layouts, whether for a new moon, full moon, life crisis, transformation, career change, or kids. Then things got intuitive *and so fun.* It began about five years ago as I started to deeply explore my intuition and insight. I remember the first time I consciously followed my heart and third eye through every step of the reading.

I was shuffling my oracle cards, and I couldn't decide on just one situation to focus on; I had so many questions to explore. So, I left it all up to Spirit. As I was looking at the cards, I heard "five." I spread all the cards out, facedown, and chose the five that stood out the most.

I tapped on the first one, and I knew it was about my career. I turned it over, and before I looked in the guidebook, I wrote down everything that came to me when I connected with the image on the card. Once I had read the accompanying book, I was profoundly moved by the words of advice around my career that spoke to me deeply.

I tapped on the second card and knew it was about my kids. The third card was insight into my marriage. The fourth card was about my health. And the fifth was clarity around friendships.

With each card, I followed the same steps as with my first card. I had a wealth of inspired insight to write down; I was joyfully inundated and in the flow with the cards like never before. Now when I'm doing something like this intuitively, I'm completely aligned and deeply connected with my Soul and the process.

I didn't let doubt trip me up for a second; I was too deliciously intertwined in the beautiful reading that provided so much relief, healing, and encouragement for me in many areas of my life.

· PRACTICE ·
Create Your Own Reading

A gentle word of caution before you begin: I wholeheartedly advise you to avoid contacting Spirit—through cards or other ways—when you are feeling angry, exhausted, or depleted, affected by alcohol or drugs, or otherwise not present and calm. Don't do it to show off or be popular. Don't do it to play with the dark energies. Connect with a positive intention, when you're clearheaded, with grace and gratitude always. If your energy is low and you need help from Spirit, contact the Archangels and Ascended Masters or your own personal Spirit Guides. Call in love to light the way before you begin and always honor your inner wisdom.

I encourage you to choose a set of cards that ignite deep joy. Find a quiet place, light a candle if you wish, make a pot of tea, perhaps find a crystal or sacred object that wants to sit with you, and relax. Close your eyes for a minute and imagine a swirl of white light all around you, holding the highest intention for your reading. Once you feel settled, let your Soul and Divine Team guide you to create a richly informative and rewarding layout.

1. Choose the deck of cards that you're most excited about playing with.

2. Shuffle the cards thoroughly, thinking about one or more subjects, questions, ideas, prospects, or just have an open heart, then spread them flat and facedown in an organic row.

3. Ask Spirit how many cards you require, then slowly choose the cards that energetically jump out or the ones that feel warm or tingly under your hand.

4. Keep them facedown and turn them over one at a time. Let the cards speak to your heart first before you look up the

meaning. Soak up the guidance completely before you flip over the next card.

5. Write it all down. Keep an oracle and tarot journal so you can look back on each reading when you want to be inspired by your own journey.

6. When you're finished, give thanks to Spirit, the cards, and your amazing Highest Self.

If you're not feeling aligned with or excited by the readings you're receiving from a particular deck, you might want to clear it with sage, place it in the beams of a full moon, or send it refreshing white light with the intention of clearing the energy within it. This is also how I clear cards that friends have been playing with.

Trust yourself. Never put a card back or start over again because you don't think it was right. It's right the first go. Always.

Chapter 7

TRUST

"As soon as you trust yourself, you will know how to live."
—JOHANN WOLFGANG VON GOETHE

As significant as it is to connect within, without trust, there's no impact. Live your life with faith in your own wild wisdom, certain that you know what is right for you, committed to and confident in your worth, and hopeful that you will forge the most abundant path according to your highest good. Trust is invaluable in aligning you with your Soul. In this chapter, I'll pour out my stories, my biggest lessons, and all I've learned about trusting in me.

Cultivating Trust in My Knowing

It was a stunning Saturday afternoon in May 2017, less than a week after my fortieth birthday. I was standing on the side of an active Californian volcano, ankle-deep in snow, eyes closed, soaking up the overwhelmingly delicious and unmistakably healing rush of energy flowing through me as I stood in the center of a powerful energy vortex.

I'd spent the morning walking through the sacred sites of Mount Shasta, and although I was a long way from where I lived, I felt right at home. Now here I was, in one of the most potent places on earth. After I'd been in the vortex for a little while, my guide, Ashalyn, asked me if I was done. I opened my eyes, smiled, and said yes.

"No, you're not," she said. "There's a being of light about ten feet behind you."

"Who is it?" I asked.

She gave me a look I'd already seen many times that day. Even though we had only met that morning, I'd spent enough time with Ashalyn to know what her eyes were saying. I knew from her silence—and raised eyebrow—that I still didn't trust myself. I was still giving my power away. I was still scared of tuning in, sharing my answers, and risking being wrong. I was standing on the edge of a goddamn volcano with all the forces of Mother Nature coursing through my body and I was *still* unsure of myself.

I closed my eyes and opened my palms to receive wisdom from Spirit. With fresh determination and grit, I tuned in to the being behind me.

"Grandma!" I shouted.

Ashalyn smiled.

Immediately I felt the love of my Mama's Mama. A beautiful woman I'd barely known as a child but had felt her guidance in spirit for many years, ever since my Mama's youngest sister sent me Grandma's gold ring.

"My darling girl, I'm so proud of you for everything, for being who you are, for following your heart to Mount Shasta, and for being brave," Grandma told me. "Now will you please stop giving yourself a hard time for *everything*; perfectionism is hurting you."

I smiled a big wide smile of understanding and acknowledgment. I nodded, grateful and giddy. And then I cried. I bawled for a solid fifteen minutes; I cried so hard, so ugly, and so loud. My whole body shook. My knees gave way. When Ashalyn checked in on me, I couldn't stop the saltwater stream to speak. I went on crying until I was done.

When I was finished, when the healing was through, I explained to Ashalyn that the day I took home Grandma's resized ring from the jeweler, she came to me in the form of the song "Truly, Madly, Deeply," by Savage Garden, on the radio. I pulled the car over to the side of the road, covered in goose bumps, and for the first time ever, I just *knew* a song was sent to me from the other side.

The lyrics speak of mountains, oceans, and lying on the earth under falling stars. Over the years, I'd felt Grandma's strong and healing presence when I was floating in the ocean on holidays, bathing in the sea, and now here she was right next to me while I stood on one of the world's most breathtaking mountains. The perfection of the moment blew me sideways. (Since then, I've felt her close to me on a trip to the country where I made a medicine drum. One night the stars were so vivid and thick, it appeared they were falling down on me. She was totally there, too. Nice one, Grandma.)

If those tears had any emotional substance to them, if there was something that I was shedding in the salty lakes that pooled and froze at my feet, it was doubt. Because ever since that moment, I have trusted myself like never before. I'm not perfect, but I have honored my intuition daily. Of that, I am wildly proud.

I trust in me. I trust in my spirit. I trust that my path will be clear when I need to know the next step. I trust that I have a gilded purpose. I trust that I will know when to speak my truth. I trust that I am taken care of and I am safe. I trust that love will guide me home.

That's a lot of trust to cultivate, but when doubt has been cleared, there's finally space for trust to enter. If doubt does show up uninvited, it doesn't last long around here.

Mount Shasta, Ashalyn, and my gorgeous Grandma changed me forever. Now I believe in me.

LIMITLESS BEINGS RIDE THEIR OWN WAVE

Limitless beings, such as yourself, are incapable of thriving within limits. Yet, here we are; oversaturated, overinsulted, overpreached, overinformed, overshamed, overinstructed, overexposed, overcriticized, and overwhelmed by the rights and wrongs, the dos and do nots, the rules of living in a restrictive box ... when we're the same shape and form as the ocean.

We're fluid and wild, boundless and vital. We're not meant to be contained. Trusting ourselves is an impossible task if we have no say in the direction of our lives. Trust can only be cultivated from taking a step in faith and knowing that we cannot fail, that our truth is the most important mentor as we walk our path.

You don't need to buy into anyone else's fears or ideas. Not your parent's. Not your teacher's. Not your doctor's. Not your guru's. Not your partner's. Not your boss's. Not the media's. The only person to trust completely is you, sweet Soul. You are not responsible for what has happened to you, but you are responsible for how you act, react, think, speak, and feel. Know your values. Let them be fluid. Sync them with your heart.

Go ahead, wild ocean, and soak up the advice of ten thousand gurus and guides, books and movies, lovers and seekers, mentors and teachers—but at the end of the day, you need to trust that you alone have the final say in your life, and that your final say is perfect and worthy and good.

Your intuition will show you what advice, guidance, and wisdom is meant for you at this time. Your instinct will tell you when to walk away. Your insight will light up your path with the possibility of new ideas. Trust in your vastness. Be an ocean of love for the world.

TRUST INVOLVES PATIENCE AND COURAGE

My Soul sister Hanna has learned a lot about trust in her life, particularly when it comes to living intuitively. She told me a story recently about finding her place in the world that brought a huge smile to my face. Hanna grew up in Poland and moved to England for six years when she was a young adult. In England, she was settled and mostly happy. She had an amazing career, a long-term relationship, and a wonderful circle of friends.

But there was always an inner, uncomfortable niggle, like she wasn't properly at home yet. Her Soul never felt as expansive or fulfilled as she had hoped. Something was missing, but she had no idea what it looked like.

One day, she was guided into a very deep meditation with a mentor to discover her place in the world. She saw images of a beautiful, warm, and sunny country with gorgeous nature and animals. With a pounding and expansive heart, she knew ... *this was home*. When the session was over, she had no clue what to do, but a few days later, serendipity stepped in. Images of Australia came up "randomly" on her computer, images that had the same resonance as the place in her meditation. Her heart knew; her intuition was calling her home. She had felt the truth and she couldn't turn her back on it.

"It wasn't easy," she told me, "but every day I woke up with that feeling in my heart. There was no day or night when I didn't feel the urge to go to this country to see it. The journey was very difficult because my parents didn't support me, most of my friends couldn't understand why I was doing this, I had to finish my relationship because my boyfriend didn't want to come with me, and my career had to be dealt with."

It took two years to make the move, but she's never had a single regret. "I put my foot on this land and I knew straight away in my heart that I'm in the right place. I instantly experienced a deep feeling of peace, happiness, and fulfillment I had never known before—and it is with me every single day. This is my home. Every day is a blessing. It's the best decision of my life. The hardest, too, but the most rewarding. I'm so grateful for my intuition, courage, and faith. The more I live in my truth, the easier life flows and the more amazing people I meet. People help me a lot on my journey, and often it feels like I am meeting angels."

Hanna has been shining her light in Australia now for seven years. She's met her Soul mate, whom she is now married to, works with native animals, lives near the beach, and radiates her inner sunshine for miles around.

Charging your heart with hope instead of self-doubt makes the journey of self-awareness a sparkling one. But for many, it's not easy. Perhaps someone you loved repeatedly doubted you. Perhaps you were not completely trusted by a parent, guardian, teacher, or partner; they may have controlled, disregarded, or even ignored your desires. When the people we love and admire show us they don't trust us, we often fall into line with their beliefs and take them on as our own. It's less painful this way. We mistakenly think this is the safest route. Over time, our self-trust weakens, we're not sure if we're "right" or trustworthy enough to speak our truth, and we look to others for advice that we could easily give ourselves, if only we could depend on the contents of our hearts.

I felt the heavy, vacuous feeling of obsessive self-doubt for many years. For me, the worst part was the suspicion, confusion, and inadequacy within, even when it was clear that other people around me thought I was courageous and living my truth. I have met amazing friends, been promoted many times at work, traveled solo in countless countries, been lucky in love, birthed two brilliant beings, and run my own successful business, but still there has been a lot of self-doubt, like I didn't deserve my life and I didn't trust myself to not mess it all up. Thank goodness it is greatly diminished these days.

Self-doubt is exhausting. Always unsure of yourself, your feet never really hit the ground with confidence, you never fully relax, and you've always got something to prove so no one discovers how "wrong" you really are.

I find self-doubt to be the product of an overactive ego that has been handed a loudspeaker. The ego, instinct, and trust all have a close relationship. When your instinct isn't grounded in security, when your gut is hurting, you may begin to feel vulnerable, and that's when the ego tries to step all over your fire. Nourish your gut, heal your ancestral lineage, bless your family, meditate, find a chakra healer—do whatever your gut is asking you to do for healing. When you can see beneath this false sense of unworthiness and uncover what has brought this unease into being, you will experience a powerful level of healing that will strengthen your instinct and give rise to a stronger foundation of confidence within.

You were born worthy, and you are the one with the answers. Fall gently into trust. There's no force needed to trust yourself; force will only get in the way. Simply allow trust to be part of how you live, and you will experience a deep worthiness, hope, and self-confidence within you.

Calling In Personal Power

Self-trust is a crucial part of cultivating personal power. Trusting excessively in others is giving your power away, while trusting yourself is keeping your power within, like a fire that burns strong.

Chronically looking to other people for advice, validation, permission, and acceptance is constantly giving your power away. When you're always focused externally, slowly you lose the capacity to think, act, or create for yourself because you've forgotten who you really are and what you truly desire. The ego loves this way of living; it loves having external identities to rely on. It doesn't want you to think for yourself because that's way too risky.

This way of living may drive you to value possessions because you're not tuned inward, so you're continuously looking for meaning outside yourself. Meaning can never be found externally, because that's not where it lives. If left unchecked, these kinds of cravings will only get more intense. You'll need more things to attempt to satisfy this bottomless desire or addictions may arise in order to numb the pain of your unheard truth.

What your Soul genuinely craves is an unshakeable connection within. When you tune in to your intuitive heart, you begin to live life from an empowered and internal focus. You get curious about the ideas of others whom you admire, but in the end, you go your own way. You make your own rules. You design your own spirituality. You eat food that feels right to you. You connect with people who feel good to you. You speak your truth when you need to. You create meaning in the small moments of mindful magic. You take time to find out who you want to become, and you devote and prioritize your time accordingly. *This is how you do you*. And this is how you develop a strong sense of trust in yourself, by aligning with your intuitive vehicle and noticing how far it takes you along the slipstream of life.

The more internally focused you become, the more you lose those shallow external identities that your ego has been hooked into. You become genuinely free as you come back home to your Soul. You learn that the risks you took in simply and honestly being yourself weren't as scary as your ego tricked you into thinking they would be.

Sacred being, love and trust yourself exactly as you are: a *Soul*, created by Great Spirit, made of light and love; a *body*, a wondrous work of art, with all its curves and beauty, that you chose before you were born; a *mind*, as clever as any other, with gifts and talents and the ability to achieve anything you desire; and a *spirit*, a never-ending energy that pulsates within and around your being, touching all you connect with.

To be clear, this isn't about *not* trusting anyone else. This is about trusting *you first*.

· RITUAL ·
Affirmations for Self-Empowerment

To cultivate more trust in your heart, try these affirmations. I recommend writing your own if the inspiration comes to you and placing them somewhere obvious and meaningful. If one of them feels really powerful when you say it out loud, it's a message for you to open up to the energy of the words as deeply as possible. Don't rush these; say them out loud and let the energy of the words linger. Tune in to the feeling of each of them to amplify their activation within you.

- I have the wisdom of many lives and the ancient ones in my Soul.
- I trust that I know what is true, helpful, and nourishing for me.
- I consciously create the adventure of my dreams every day.

- I adore myself and regularly take time to listen to my wants and needs.

- I am my own wise guru. I bow at my own altar. I wholeheartedly respect my wishes.

- I am here on this planet for an important reason. I allow my purpose to unfold daily.

- I am worthy of abundance, peace, money, freedom, love, and living life on my own terms.

- I cherish my pure connection to the cosmos every day.

FRIENDS ARE THE GUARDIANS OF OUR HEARTS

There's no safer place in the world than a group of friends who love, respect, accept, and honor your uniqueness, authenticity, and truth. People who embrace the evolution, experience, and expression of *you*.

Finding my Soul sisters and brothers has been an adventure in trust. The more I know and respect myself, the more likely I am to attract those who respect me as I am. The more I trust others and allow them to depend on me, the more sumptuous and vibrant the experience of friendship becomes.

I've created many friendships in the past from a place of shallow self-worth and trust. I've been draining, intimidating, anxious, fake, needy, or too pleasing. The people whom I connected with on this level didn't respect me because I didn't respect myself. These friendships were rarely genuine or real because they weren't based on my truth. Only a few friends who saw through the façade to the real me stuck close and stayed awhile.

That's how it is with friendships. Start with an open and honest heart and choose those who *feel* good, and you'll receive back whatever you give. Listen to your gut when it tells you to stay away. You don't need to fix people. You don't need to be everyone's friend. Just move toward those who are meant for you.

We all change, we all grow, we all have different wants and needs. Trust a handful of aligned friends. Without trust, your relationships won't deepen or expand to their full potential. Allow space for arguments. Expect times of silence and separation. Some will turn their back on you; bless them. Others will gossip about you; forgive them. Stay strong in your light and don't take it personally.

Find the true friends with whom you can have mindful conversations, delicious adventures, wild holidays, long hugs, longer lunches, and sacred times. Connect hand to heart. Never fear the uncertainty; it'll keep you anxious, lonely, and disconnected.

Friends will hold space for you to be unashamedly real. To be honest about *everything*. Find solace in communities who are navigating this journey of a lifetime in their own way, who have their own beliefs that may differ completely from your own, and who wish to share their wisdom from their own honest and unique perspective. If you can trust that you're okay to be wholly you, then you'll create space for others to be safely and completely themselves.

By being around others who are in touch with themselves, you'll also become more in tune with yourself. By connecting with brothers and sisters who love to laugh, you'll rediscover your own rapturous laughter. It doesn't have to be profound truth-talking all the time. Sitting silently, shoulder to shoulder through a movie is calm connection. Talking about life over a good pizza is joyous connection. Bushwalking together is natural connection. Making music together is harmonious connection. Browsing your local markets together is adventurous connection. Meet with others in a way where you can really enjoy *being* together.

There may be periods in your life when you won't have a close friend, or a tight community, or a regular dinner date. Friends come and go. And that's okay. There's a cycle and a season for everything and everyone. Take time to celebrate those who are in your life at this moment, those who lift you higher, those who honor your trust and trust you right back. These people are the guardians of your heart.

My friend Erin is a beautiful, empathic introvert who often finds it difficult to make new friends. She does, however, have a circle of women around her whom she has intuitively connected with along her journey, and for each of them, she is so grateful.

One friend in particular was a huge surprise from the universe. Shortly before falling pregnant with her first child, Erin was scrolling through her Facebook feed when she saw a post from a woman she didn't know, asking if anyone in Erin's local area would be interested in joining a group fitness training session. This kind of post had never, *ever* piqued Erin's interest, but a little voice inside her prompted her to *just say yes*.

It turned out this woman wasn't your average personal trainer; she set intentions before classes and meditated at the end. She helped Erin through her pregnancy and prepared her physically for labor. She taught self-love and intuition and how to trust your body as much as your inner voice.

Erin is stoked that she trusted her heart's nudge. Even though it led her out of her comfort zone, it took her into a more expansive zone. Because she learned to trust in her knowing in a whole new and empowered way, she found another guardian for her heart, one who inspires her to be intuitively healthy every day.

PRESENCE AND GRATITUDE

My morning meditations are wild and sovereign. Quiet mornings are a powerful time for me to receive messages, love, support, and Soul-quenching nourishment. If I skip this precious time of connecting with Spirit and the rising sun, I'll usually attempt to rush headfirst into the day with blurry eyes and ungrounded roots.

When I open to my inner counsel as a daily priority to check in, accept, and trust that I have the love and the answers, the therapy and the desires, all perfectly within my inner universe, then I create a deeper communion with myself. I learn to trust my heart before I ask anyone else.

To become more self-aware and trust what that awareness leads to, take up more space and nourish your presence. Question everything. Tune in to your thoughts, your body, your emotions, your energy, and the environment all around you. This is a gentle, moment-to-moment process that allows guidance to unfold from within. And when you add gratitude, it truly comes alive.

Self-awareness blooms simply, softly, and gently. With trust, it stays nourished. With presence and gratitude, it flourishes. With patience, you'll reap beautifully what you wholeheartedly sow.

In time, you'll trust your spirit, dreams, friendships, visions, unknown, magic, and the whole wild dance of consciously awakening.

· PRACTICE ·
Self-Trust Soul Prompts

Try these questions to deepen your devotion and confidence in yourself. I encourage you to keep a positive focus and not dwell on the negative aspects. Your ego may wish to use this exercise as a way of bringing down your energy (as it doesn't feel safe around high energy), but if you stay focused on curiosity, self-love, and compassion, the answers will flow through you.

In what ways do you feel like you're being limited in your expression? Who is limiting you and why have you been allowing it? Or have you been limiting yourself with old programs in your unconscious mind? What can you do to set free your most unapologetic and full expression?

Where in your life are you weighed down with doubt? What about yourself are you doubting? How can you let this doubt go?

How does it feel to trust yourself? How does it feel for you to trust in the universe? How is your heart guiding you to trust in life with open arms?

Can you see all the ways in which you've trusted yourself over the last week? Write them down. Acknowledge these moments. Often it takes a moment of acknowledgment to appreciate all you've done and all you're capable of doing.

SURRENDERING DOUBT AND EMBRACING CONFIDENCE

Whenever I notice myself thinking or saying, "I don't know," I pause for a moment, take a deep breath, surrender the doubt, and try again. Because I *do* know. Perhaps I need time to find the answer. Maybe I need a moment to myself to go a little deeper. I might need a cup of tea, a few oracle cards, twenty minutes with my journal, a walk in nature, or a long, lush bath. But I *will* find the answer.

I am so grateful for the level of trust I have in my heart and knowing, body and energy, Spirit Guides and angels, lineage and past lives, and all the ways in which I'm able to find the answer … no matter the question.

I'm also happy to ask for help—should it be an extra-tricky question with a twist—from my husband, family, friends, healers, psychics, psychologists, or whoever I think might be able to help. But I always give my intuition a chance to dig deep and answer first. Because even if I don't have the optimal answer within, I'll at least sense the direction to pursue.

I'm the kind of person who doesn't like to be wrong, which is why I used to have such an ingrained habit of saying, "I don't know." It felt safer than guessing and getting the wrong answer. I thought it was an honest admission of my level of understanding, but really it was a lukewarm answer from an insecure perfectionist. I'm not short on information, magic, opinions, research, connections, or ideas, so I no longer shy away from sharing them with others (without being the oversharing know-it-all of my twenties). The truth is, I doubted my Soul's knowing, which was slowly being choked into submission by doubt, fear, and unworthiness.

Trusting myself had everything to do with feeling worthy. If I didn't feel worthy of being a mum, wife, friend, writer, healer, mentor, and speaker, then I would be ineffective in my capacity in those areas. When I got clear that I was worthy of all those ways of being—because I'm simply and profoundly *alive*—trust paved the way for me to own them to the best of my ability.

Trust is a delicate strength. It requires attention—gentle, eternal, loyal attention. And reverence. Trust your inner wisdom and give it some major airtime. Trust in the perception of your Soul.

· RITUAL ·
Intuitive Muscle Testing

Muscle testing has been around for a long time. It's the backbone to kinesiology, and it's been scientifically shown to work accurately and with ease. I've been taught by a spiritual mentor to use it as a powerful tool to help me when I need answers directly from my divinely connected energy.

I want to share this with you because it has been extraordinarily helpful on my path. I regularly use this particular technique, but I always tune in to my knowing first. I trust my inner guidance, but sometimes I need a little backup.

Here are four tips before you start:

1. *Be present.* Try not to do this while on the run, driving, dehydrated, upset, overwhelmed, intoxicated, or otherwise disengaged or distracted.

2. *Be focused.* Tune in to the person, subject, or situation with clarity, or ask your Highest Self or a Spirit Guide. Focus with your mind on exactly *what* you want to know and *who* you're asking. Be clinical; try to remove your preferences and personal inclinations. When in doubt, ask that consciousness guide your answers.

3. *Be specific.* A vague question will give you a vague answer. Be as detailed as possible.

4. *Be reverent.* The universe doesn't favor those who show off their spiritual "tricks" with the wrong intention. This is a sacred method to access guidance and trust.

Here are three steps to muscle test with ease:

1. Take your left thumb and connect it to your left middle finger to create a circle. Do the same with your right hand. Open one circle slightly to loop these two circles together, then close them together. You want your connection to be firm but not too strong.

2. Now that you've created your chain, ask your body to show you a "yes," then try pulling your hands apart where the fingers meet. Then ask your body to show you a "no," and try again. A "yes" should feel strong, like you can't break the chain. A "no" tends to be weaker, like you can't hold the chain. This is because muscles are weaker in a negative response. You may have the opposite responses—accept and trust them however they are for you. If this isn't crystal clear, have a drink of water, take a deep breath, focus a little more, and try again.

3. Now that you have easy access to your body's wisdom, you can try this in whatever setting you wish. Clear your mind, focus on your question, and trust the answer.

I use this technique a few times a week, but I don't rely on it as my main source of wisdom. I go with my heart and only use this as a tool to clarify an answer or if my surroundings are too distracting, noisy, or confusing for me to tune in.

Personally, I'll use this technique if I need to tune in to the particular energy of a restaurant when choosing a healthy place for dinner, a hotel that suits my holistic needs, a book that fulfills my desires, a course that will guide me to a greater knowing in what I desire to learn, a remedy for a particular symptom or illness, a healer for my highest good, or a practitioner that aligns with my needs. I'll use muscle testing when I need to get out of my mind's chatter and make the highest possible decision.

Trust in all that you are, all that you know, and all that you are given. When you feel the nudges and whispers, feelings and synchronicities, truth and direction … trust in your heart.

Chapter 8

HONOR

"Honor is self-esteem made visible in action."

—AYN RAND

Honoring yourself is intuition in motion. To honor yourself is to follow through with what you receive from your inner guidance, a valuable step that too many people miss because they're still unsure or doubting what they hear. If you don't trust yourself, you won't be able to fully honor yourself either. Honoring yourself is showing up for all of it. It's activating your ideas, sparking magic from your gifts, and sharing your heart with the world.

HONOR YOUR TRUTH

As you connect to the deepest parts of your intuitive self, you'll have two choices. The first is to doubt and ignore what your inner wisdom is telling you, to go on pretending it doesn't matter or that you're not worthy, clever, or spiritual enough to live an abundant and wholehearted life. The second choice is to honor it, to bravely heed the call and do what you *know* you need to do. To say *yes* to your spirit, your path and purpose, the hard-won wisdom of your ancestors and past lives, the guidance of your body, your energetic feedback, your inner truth, and your Divine Team. To honor your

179

intuition is to take an audacious step in the direction of your bliss, your dreams, your magic, and your burning desires.

You now know where your inner wisdom lives and what it's all about. You've breathed new energy into your lifeforce, surrendered your fears, made a profound connection with yourself and your cosmic helpers, and built up a foundation of trust in yourself. Now here you are, free to live a life of your choosing. All you have to do is honor yourself.

This takes grit, patience, courage, and unflinching self-love. But when you honor what you know to be true for you, rather than living by default, you get to follow your heart toward the life you were meant to live. Remember, the ego loves to play small, to be predictable, and to keep things the same. Don't resist this; just let it go. Let go of the ego's false fears and disguises—let it dissolve by honoring love again and again.

· PRACTICE ·
Authentic Wisdom Soul Prompts

Start by taking three deep belly breaths. Surrender any tension. When you call your power back, you're bringing any scattered energy back into your whole self so that you can feel complete exactly as you are. Say, "I call my power back. I call my power back. I call my power back. I am healing and whole, complete and entirely me. And so it is."

Now it's time to get curious about what your Highest Self wants you to honor. If you don't sense any answers straight away, let the questions sit with you and see what you discover throughout the day (or what insight your dreams bring you at night). There's no rush to any of this; let the wisdom come in its own time.

If you trusted the wisdom of your body completely, what would you do to honor the messages from your body? Where in your body are the strongest messages coming from?

Where is your Soul directing you? How will you honor the wise guidance of your Soul?

What is the counsel of your heart yearning to tell you in this moment? How will you honor the wholehearted wisdom from deep within your being?

What are the highest thoughts in your mind? How will you stay close to love and high-vibrational thoughts?

How does your spirit wish for you to express yourself more authentically?

In what ways does your Highest Self wish for you to care for the world? How will you honor your purpose today?

Follow Your Bliss

Having dreams in the pipeline of life will give you joy, satisfaction, and a journey to pursue. If you are in a dream drought, then you may feel lethargic, depressed, confused, or purposeless. If you have a selection of dreams close by to work on, then you can dip in and out of them, trusting that the right ones will come to fruition and the others, even if they fall away, will serve a higher purpose, too. Honoring dreams is taught by many to be "selfish," but they were planted in your Soul before you incarnated and need to be tended to in this life to weave your highest purpose together.

But how do you create a dream, honor it, and bring it to life? You follow your bliss.

Bliss is a feeling of being lit up from the center of your being. A sensation of openness, ease, and unbounded joy. It's a feeling that goes above and beyond words to show you the way.

Think of bliss as the high vibes that you feel around a certain idea, person, or situation that is so right for you. Low vibes or feelings of discomfort, tension, or unease are showing you that something isn't right for you, even if your ego is trying to convince you otherwise. Following your bliss means leaning toward anything that feels expansive and true, be it words, ideas, jobs, adventure, clothes, opinions, food, books, friends, or anything that lights you up.

Joseph Campbell famously encouraged the world to follow their bliss. Personally, I've found the deepest bliss in the simplest moments, such as a morning cup of warm cacao, a sublime stroll in nature, a gentle yoga class, a silly drawing session with my kids, deliciously soulful music, a scrumptious snack, or a belly laugh with my husband. Little blissful moments throughout the day make for an enormously happy life *and* they pave the way for fresh insights to drop in and create a ripple effect in your life.

When you open up to mindful bliss, you'll naturally call in some bold, blissful dreams, too. Such as changing jobs, enrolling in a course, moving to a new neighborhood, starting or ending a relationship, finding new friends or leaving old ones, changing what you eat, deepening your spiritual practice, and expanding your life.

Some days life calls you to take a small step toward your dreams; other days you'll feel the pull to do something major. Your heart is guiding you toward your bliss every minute of the day. Honor it. Whatever it asks you to do, wherever it tells you to go, however it wants you to live, honor it. You have nothing to fear, nothing to lose (except things that aren't meant for you anyway), and a life of joyous purpose to gain.

Honoring your heart doesn't mean you have to do anything that you don't want to do. Your intuition simply wants you to be true to you. Your Soul wants you to be happy and living life abundantly on your terms.

Intuitive living doesn't mean feeling wildly happy all the time. There will be moments when you'll need to express anger, move through the depths of grief, feel intense frustration, let yourself be irritated, and generally be present to any shadowy emotions that arise. Feel into your shadow when it comes, but don't lose yourself in the back of it. When you've honored your pain, step back into the light, and look intuitively for the signs guiding you back to love.

Following are some prompts specifically created to pair with your morning and evening rituals.

· PRACTICE ·
Inspired Morning Questions

The energy of the morning is sweetly serene. As you slowly wake from your sleep, your mind is in between worlds and largely connected to Spirit. This is a potent time to check in with your inner awareness and wisdom, to allow messages from your Soul to flow through you. Try these questions or write whatever comes to mind from your dreamy mind.

- What did your dream state want to share with you last night? How did your dreams feel? Were there any messages?
- How does your heart feel today? Do you need to bring in more love, deep breaths, self-care, or wonder before you start the day?
- What would refresh your energy this morning? What can you do to honor your energy?
- What is your intention for this day? Set a positive intention around how you want to feel.

- How can you honor your Soul's guidance? What is your Soul telling you as you rise into a fresh new day? How can you acknowledge who you are today?
- How open is your heart to bliss, wonder, and serendipity? Is there anything that would help open it even more?

· PRACTICE ·
Contemplative Evening Questions

Each day we take a lot of our stress into the bedroom, which messes with such a sacred space and can contribute to poor sleep. By journaling at night and relieving the tension from your day, you let the negative vibes float off you, so you feel lighter when it comes to bedtime. Use these questions or let your heart flood the page with thoughts from your day.

- How were you guided today by your inner wisdom? How did you honor it, and how did that feel?
- What did you do that brought you into or out of flow? What felt aligned and what didn't?
- What did you wholeheartedly do today that you would like to acknowledge? How can you celebrate your connection to your Higher Self?
- What are you aware of about yourself that you weren't aware of yesterday?
- What is your intention for this night? Would you like to receive any guidance from your dreams?
- How will you honor your body's rhythms and prepare yourself for sleep?

Embracing Unexpected Plot Twists

For years I longed to learn Reiki energy healing, though I wasn't sure why. I loved having Reiki as a treatment, but I also loved massages and never longed to be a masseuse. I've been a writer my whole life, so following the nudges to write have always felt aligned, but I never considered myself to be a healer, so I didn't understand the pull to learn Reiki.

However, when I thought about my kids, the idea of having a deeper understanding of energy healing for them deepened my cravings to learn Reiki. I've done a course in homeopathy just so I could confidently administer homeopathic remedies to my kids and myself, and homeopathy has been a gift to our whole family, so I decided I'd do the same with Reiki.

In 2017, I studied Reiki I and Reiki II with two different teachers. By the end of the second course, I had experienced such a profound healing within me, I knew there would be more to this practice than just using it on the kids. The day after the second course, my friend Lu sent me a message asking for healing for herself and her beloved dog. I wasn't expecting to tap into my new abilities straight away, but this was clearly divine timing, a gilded opportunity that I wasn't going to miss. I needed to honor what felt right, even if it stretched me out of my comfort zone.

While healing my sweet friend Lu and her dog, I saw visions, movies, colors, energy, and lights. Angels and messages came to me clearly. I was given food advice, wellness ideas, and tips for their happiness. I had never felt so psychically alive in my life. I felt like something had opened up through my Reiki training, like the double French doors to my Soul were thrown open and suddenly there was a new view, a fresh breeze moving through me, and a perspective on life that was so kickass in its vibrancy.

If I had let labels and preconceived ideas of my career or abilities set my limitations, then I would have resisted Reiki because I didn't identify as a "healer." But now I have the powerful and pleasurable gift of Reiki healing to offer friends, family, and clients all over the world. It gives me feelings of satisfaction, wonder, delight, purpose, and free-flowing bliss.

I'm amazed at the magic that has poured into my life since learning Reiki. It feels like sacred magnetism at work. And all because I honored the inner pull and trusted that wherever it was taking me was going to be for my highest benefit.

Honor Your Cosmic Talents

My close friend Ros is such an inspiration to me. Not only is she enormously kind and talented, but she's always been so creative with her life purpose. When she was pregnant with her first child, she felt a vivid knowing that her career in human resources was nearing its organic conclusion and that something more fulfilling was around the corner.

Her Soul kept hinting that she needed to complete her qualification in remedial massage that she had started eight years prior. It wasn't something that made sense to her logical brain or fearful, doubting, limited ego, but eventually, once she had two children and felt ready to work again, she finished her diploma and a new career fell swiftly and abundantly into place.

After five years of working as a massage therapist in a busy clinic, her Soul once more showed her a new direction. She diligently honored the call, quit the practice, and set up her own healing room at home, incorporating a more spiritual and energetic element into her healing work. Again, her ego wasn't thrilled at the initial loss of income, but this step opened her up to opportunities and avenues that she couldn't have accessed had she stayed at the clinic.

It was at this time that we met and became fast friends, and it didn't take me long to book in with her for a treatment. Her astonishing talents and cosmic gifts radiated through my energy field and the whole room. This was the first time I'd experienced Reiki in such a healing and meaningful way, and it was because Ros had honored her heart that I was able to tap into my own intuitive pull. Thanks to that hour of bliss, I realized my yearning to learn Reiki for myself, which has been one of my greatest gifts. And all because my Soul sister followed her bliss.

The trust you put in yourself emanates from you and inspires others to trust themselves. The way you honor your heart excites others to honor the wild wisdom in theirs. Everything has a vibrational ripple effect that you cannot ever see or fathom. Keep honoring yourself, intuitive one. You're making a difference with every sacred step.

Unraveling Your Soul Purpose

I don't believe you can ever *discover* your Soul's purpose so much as unravel it, thread by thread. Your purpose is in you all along. It's something you remember day by day, bliss by bliss.

I never imagined the full extent of my Soul's purpose until I finally took a good, conscious look inside my heart. When I saw what I really wanted—to write professionally—I decided to give it a go, even though I didn't have a degree in journalism, and I was almost thirty years old. I had been writing in notebooks my whole life, and besides food, there was nothing else I would rather talk about than books and stories, prose and language. I figured I would land where I was meant to be, so I aimed for the moon.

I spent my twenties searching for purpose, moving from one job to the next. Some jobs I held for three months, others for three years, and even though I adored most of the positions I had, I was never completely satisfied. I was restless. I wanted more. The universe beckoned me onward.

Looking back, I can see this was the gentle urging of my spirit to keep moving on. To learn and grow and try something new so I could unravel more and more of my unique spark and purpose. I kept moving, trying, learning, connecting, and playing with different careers.

I worked various jobs in restaurants: waitress, host, food runner, cashier, barista, bartender, and manager. I worked as a corporate catering manager and a retail manager of a stunning upmarket food provedore. After all this time in the food industry, I needed a break. I knew that there was something else out there for me, but I didn't know what that looked like yet.

With every job I met new people, some of whom I would connect with so deeply, the job seemingly didn't matter at all. And every job, no matter how easy or challenging it was, brought lessons, gifts, rewards, and a brighter understanding of my true self. Nothing was a waste.

It wasn't until I decided to have a go at writing that I landed a dream job. I'd been working in media as a personal assistant, advertising coordinator, and editorial coordinator, soaking up the frantically and intoxicatingly creative world of magazines. When the job of Beauty and Health editor at *Real Living* magazine became available, I went for it. I was already working at the magazine—and in love with the team. It was like nothing I'd ever done, yet everything had led me to that point. My bachelor's degree in psychology and sociology gave me a firm understanding of in-depth writing and a curiosity for the workings of people's minds and behaviors.

My years in hospitality and retail gave me an understanding of food and wellness. My passion for media meant that I would go the extra length to bring a feature to life.

I was so immersed in my job that for once I never questioned whether it was right for me. I didn't have to; I was living the dream. It had its challenges—really big and heavy challenges. But that job taught me so much about writing, editing, design, photography, publishing, journalism, interviewing, health, well-being, people, compassion, and inspiration.

After three years, my job was made redundant. I went on to create the most fulfilling freelancing career a girl could ask for, which I still dip into between bigger projects. Thanks to my intuition, trust, excitement, and determination, I have been published in some of the biggest magazines—in print and online—in Australia.

I began to really understand what it meant to *honor my bliss* as a freelancer. I wrote about everything that I was learning personally, all the subjects that lit me up from within, and I was published regularly. Commissions for natural health and soulful well-being features began filling my inbox. Slowly, I opened up to the idea of writing about spirituality, long before I considered myself "spiritual," simply because I was curious. More commissions came through. The universe was listening. The universe is *always* listening.

It was during this time that I realized my purpose wasn't my job. My purpose was how I lived my life. To live *on* purpose—rather than live searching for *a* purpose—felt so much more expansive and real to me. It gave me space and permission to honor whatever my purpose looked like on any given day. Because as long as I'm honoring my heart, I'm living on purpose.

Looking back at how intuitively I worked to create the kind of life and career that was true for me—sparked my creativity, served the world, brought my gifts and talents to life, and made an income—I feel wonder and joy. I see devotion. I see how I honored my inner spirit no matter what.

Everyday Service of Love

My Soul's purpose is love. Love in everyday service looks like smiling at others, helping people at every opportunity, being kind, calling friends, loving my family hard, writing to uplift others, and looking for bigger ways to heal and inspire the world.

On the days when I struggle to extend this kind of love out to the world, I give it right back to me. Smiling at myself in the mirror, thinking kind thoughts, loving my body, writing for fun, and looking for ways to heal myself.

A large part of your purpose, and your life, is about finding or creating a job that you love. A job that serves, heals, teaches, or inspires others. But your purpose is not just about doing things for others; it's how you live each day.

Intuitively honoring the cosmic path of bliss, the universal breadcrumbs of guidance, will genuinely lead you toward alignment, authenticity, joy, and purpose.

If you feel your job, relationship, or living situation isn't aligned with your Soul, it will take time to realign and consciously find your way home, and it may not always feel so blissful. Most people I know can't just stand up and walk out the door of a job, relationship, or house toward their dreams. But honestly, your intuition isn't about making fast or rushed decisions. If you listen to yourself every day, you will gradually move away from what doesn't make you truly happy and find yourself in a better place. Be patient. Have faith. Honor each moment's wisdom.

There's no need to fear change or resist growth; life requires both if it's to be fulfilling and meaningful. Yet, as you grow toward your own light, you will experience more ease and grace. As you unfurl your clench on the past and open up to the endless possibilities of the future, you will find that a new abundant flow moves through your life.

Remember, your purpose is love. Honor that, and everything else will fall into place.

BLESS YOUR WILDEST GIFTS

Without realizing it, many of us curse our gifts. We shun our sensitivities, quirks, talents, curiosities, and archetypes. We numb the loud parts of us, the whispers in the night, the fighter in us, the witch, the leader, the renegade, the psychic, the compassionate heart, the seeker of justice, the rule breaker, and the untamed mind. We're told that they're uncomfortable, awkward, inconvenient, problematic, embarrassing, humiliating, or just plain annoying. These are *all* gifts. Bless them. Honor their wild wisdom.

Other people's limiting opinions on what makes you uniquely *you* don't matter because you don't need permission from anyone to live life your way. Instead, take these inimitable qualities, embrace them, look them squarely in the eye, bless their presence, and promise them that you'll spend the rest of your life creating space to let them shine.

To be a fresh voice in a world that follows stale old rules is a *gift*. To be compassionate in an angry crowd is a *gift*. To be passionate in a passive and oppressed crowd is a *gift*. To be unexpectedly creative is a *gift*. To see, know, or feel something without reason is a *gift*. To stand up for what you believe in is a *gift*. To honor these gifts is to honor your brilliant Soul.

Live in gratitude for your spirited gifts, your rare life, and your wise intuition. Honor your weird. The brighter you shine your star, the more people who complement your kind of energy will be drawn to you. The more unique you are, the more attractive you will be to the right kind of friends, clients, and those who can add joy and abundance to your life. Honoring yourself wholeheartedly will attract others who honor you, too. People who honor you for all that you are and all that you are not and this sacred journey that you're on together.

· Practice ·
Quirky and Gifted Soul Prompts

You are a unique and brilliant being of light; there's no one like you. The more self-aware you become, the more you will realize you were not born to fit into the corners of the world. There is no mold that could possibly capture your essence in its true form. Try looking into these questions on a fresh page of your journal or spend a few minutes meditating on them.

How did your family respond to your uniqueness as a child? Did they applaud certain behaviors and ignore or put down the rest? Were you allowed to wear what you desired or express yourself in other ways?

What are you sensitive to, and how is this a gift? Are you sensitive to food, energy, sound, light, people, animals, or anything else? Keep nurturing your sensitivities and don't apologize for them. If you get a sense that they are fear-based and debilitating to your life, what kind of healer would bring your energy back to love?

What talents are you hesitant about sharing with the world? Why? We're all wildly, eccentrically, unexpectedly talented. Expressing our talents makes us feel whole and, quite often, blissfully takes us out of the ordinary world and into a higher realm. Is there a musical instrument you could borrow, a song you love to sing, a way you love to dance, an artistic creation you're wanting to try, or a style of writing you enjoy? Not all of it needs to be shared with the world, but if it's all hidden, then no one else can experience the wonder of your creativity.

What archetypes do you relate to? How can you embrace this more? The twelve Jungian archetypes are artist, innocent, sage, explorer, outlaw, magician, hero, lover, jester, everyman, caregiver, and ruler. Take your time journaling about the archetypes, for they each exist in us all in some form, and they can give you real depth of insight if you open up to them with curiosity. You might want to work with one each week as you journey deeper into self-awareness.

· RITUAL ·
Affirmations for Gratitude

These affirmations are a Soul-centered way to appreciate your life exactly as it is *and* call in more abundance and love. Manifesting begins with gratitude. Honor yourself for everything you've created in your life. Once you're finished with these, you can get more specific and give thanks for all the particulars in your life that you're grateful for. Say these out loud with one hand on your heart.

I give thanks for my wise and talented Soul that lights the way.

I give thanks for the sensual body that gives me life.

I give thanks for my curious mind that keeps me company.

I give thanks for the formidable ancestors in my bones.

I give thanks for unconditional, divine love that is always available.

I give thanks for joy that comes from listening within.

I give thanks for Mother Nature and the way nature heals and restores.

I give thanks for my uniquely fulfilling journey.

I give thanks for my bountiful gifts and flairs.

I give thanks for the universe's synchronicities.

I give thanks for all my wild emotions.

I give thanks for the freedom to be me.

I give thanks and I honor it all.

So it is.

Chapter 9

NOURISH

"My whole teaching is simply this: accept yourself, love yourself, worship yourself, celebrate yourself."

—OSHO

The previous steps to strengthen your inner connection—breathe, surrender, connect, trust, and honor—form the complete process. You've already gone wild and deep. You've journeyed inward and discovered your truth. If you've followed your intuition, you've trusted it, you've acted on it, and you now know how powerful you are. But as with everything in life, if you don't nourish it, it can't thrive. If you want to live as a sacred, self-aware creature to the best of your ability and reach your highest potential, you need to take care of you. Nourishment in any form will support the vibrant energy that weaves through all you do. Here we'll explore what it looks like to love and care for all of you.

INTUITIVELY THRIVING

When you're feeling healthy, clear, and calm, inner wisdom shines through you. Nourishing yourself without hesitation or guilt creates a foundation for genuinely abundant health and well-being.

As you look within for all the ways your being craves nourishment, you may discover that your thoughts need a little more love, your emotions are yearning to be released, your body needs different care, your energy wants to be healed, your chakras could do with some therapy, your cycles have so much to teach you, your mind is dreaming of connecting with a like-minded community, your inner child needs a hug, or your heart is craving a deeper love with your partner. That's what this final chapter is all about: giving your whole being all that you crave, desire, and need.

If the healing you require seems difficult, impossible, or too much for you to do alone, perhaps it's time to seek help. Find a practitioner, healer, coach, friend, or group who can hold space, inspire, and support you through the process.

Create as much time as possible each day for nourishment. Put it at the top of your to-do list. Self-care is not something you earn; it's something you prioritize. Nourishment is the spine of any spiritual life, and you simply cannot live or give from an empty chalice.

THE SPARK OF JOY WITHIN

Positive thoughts from loving intentions bring so much ease and depth into conscious living, healing, and growth. Whenever I find myself avoiding self-care, I come back to the story I'm telling myself around the avoidance of such rituals. I always find there's an element of fear woven into the story that needs to be unpicked and replaced with faith and love. Unpick and weave. Unpick and weave. A lifelong process.

If I'm sleeping in day after day, it's often due to a fear of not getting enough sleep. When I replace this with faith that I'll always have enough, I can rise early with ease, which creates time and space for a nourishing routine. If I'm avoiding exercise, it's usually because of a fear of feeling exhausted in the midst of an otherwise overwhelming week. When I replace this with faith that my body knows the best type of exercise to fuel me with energy and health each day, then I'm able to move more, whether it's a dance session at home or a walk along the beach.

Notice the fear, embrace it, show yourself compassion, and then create space to set a more loving intention. Come back to why you love to be nourished and how it makes you feel. One self-loving thought can wildly alter the way you create and experience your day.

Charge your positive thoughts with repetition and embodiment. Repetition gives thoughts a deeper influence on your mind by expanding them into your subconscious. Embodiment of optimism is when the body agrees with the thoughts and acts as though they are real. When you truly believe all the way through your being that you are worthy of the positive thoughts that you think, then you will begin to swiftly manifest all the goodness of your thoughts.

A positive attitude shift will expand your sense of self and cause you to act according to your highest good. These soulful actions become nurturing habits and rituals. Eventually these rituals will shape your life and have a deep impact on your unconscious beliefs and values, which drive everything you do. This is a daily process of self-love and self-belief. *This is how you change your life.*

Wake up in gratitude. Find within you a spark of joy, humility, connection, or wonder at the dawn of your day, then watch your entire day unfold with more of the same.

Make it a priority in your life to write positive affirmations, set powerful intentions, dip your pen into a gratitude journal, speak kindly, and otherwise use words for your full, creative, and compassionate expression.

Don't compare your self-care journey with others'. What you need today is different from what everyone else needs. What is easy for others may be difficult for you. Stay on your path, honor your needs, and create intentions from where you can bloom wildly.

· RITUAL ·

Everyday Self-Love Affirmations

Affirmations are one of my favorite ways of bringing a specific flavor of positivity into my life. I write affirmations in the first person (I, me, my) and always with positive words that succinctly encapsulate how I want to feel. I aim for truth and beauty, but never perfection. Say them out loud with one hand on your heart to embody the words, as though you can feel the energy of them. The more you dismiss the words as though you're "not there yet" or "not worthy of that feeling," the less impact they will have. Do your best to accept and embrace them with an open heart instead.

Here are some nourishing affirmations for you to try on, or use them to write your own:

- I am wonderfully, completely, and perfectly whole.
- My truth is a valuable light that shines freely.
- I let love guide my healing journey.
- I am open to experiencing joyful well-being every day.
- I live and breathe as one with humanity.
- I respect and honor myself as a worthy and successful individual.
- My talents come to life with every expression of creativity.
- I am gratefully responsible for my thoughts, words, and actions.

DAYDREAM OFTEN AND WELL

There has not been a single day in my life when I haven't indulged in the beautiful act of daydreaming. Daydreaming is how I get in touch with what I truly desire underneath all the expectations, "shoulds," and to-do lists. Daydreaming is how I prepare for the future with a hopeful heart.

I consider daydreaming to be valuable and nourishing. Daydreaming helps me live in a blissful state, even if just for a moment, to forget the concerns of daily life, to tune in to what brings me joy, to imagine a future that I can grow into, and to remind myself of the incredible possibilities that are available to me.

It sounds contrary to mindfulness, but as long as you're not dreaming to procrastinate or run away from your current reality, then I wholeheartedly believe it's good for your Soul.

I keep my daydreaming as close to reality as possible. I don't daydream about doing something that I have no desire to do or being someone I don't want to be. I let these accessible ideas flow so they can show me the potential of where I may go.

Daydreams inspire and excite me, and often the things I'm daydreaming about come to fruition; perhaps it's my heart's way of designing my life.

Keep your daydreams positive; use them to tell the universe about your ideal life. Anything is possible, so dream often and well. Write down your daydreams as well as your night dreams in a journal if that feels exciting to you; this can bring them to life even more tangibly. Use your conscious and unconscious dream states to understand yourself in a new way. Daydreaming is a subtle yet potent way to access your inner wisdom, as you can open your inner and outer senses in this state and allow a blissful future to find you.

Freely Expressed Emotions

Emotions are physical reactions to the environment around you; feelings are the thoughts you associate with these emotions. Emotions are the colors created by your heart, and they affect everything you feel, think, say, and do. Although they are not meant to be controlled, you are able to witness, understand, surrender, and heal your emotions more than you can imagine. Emotions create a flow of wellness, balance, and nurtured fluidity through your entire being.

When you're conscious about how you're reacting to your emotions, they become less overwhelming and more of an insight into how you're experiencing the world. Your emotions are constantly informing you from your heart and your gut, so when you tune in to the raw emotion—rather than the feeling—you are able to receive so much wisdom.

I don't expect all my emotions to feel good or to bring positive feelings into my world, but I know that they *all* have a reason for being present and they are each a gift, a portal, and a path to learning about myself on a deeper level.

Some emotions need to be expressed openly and freely, while others need a safe place to land, but usually I simply and patiently let them move through me without resisting difficult ones or attempting to hold on to the pleasant ones. Emotions themselves aren't painful; it's the resistance to or the repression of them that can be uncomfortable. Thoughts that we associate with difficult emotions can cause pain in the moment and also in the future when that emotion comes again and triggers a whole realm of unconscious memories. It sounds simple, but it works: let them flow, let them all flow.

Your inner landscape is a jungle of all kinds of emotions. When you remain mindful in the midst of any strong emotion rising, you can accept it for what it is, allow it to unfold in your being, and take on the insight it has for you. Then just let it go. This is powerfully high-vibrational living. When you notice the emotion as a part of you that is under your guidance, then you'll experience it more freely and gracefully. When you see the potential for each emotion rather than repressing or limiting it with stories, judgments, and unconscious blocks, then your energy will expand to make room for whatever needs to move through you.

Here are a few ways you can express and nourish your wild emotional state:

- *Love who you are,* love everything about you, and don't deny any emotions that surface.
- *Speak your truth,* your whole truth, in a way that empowers you and feels expansive.
- *Find healthy ways* to let the lid off your powerful emotions.
- *Look underneath strong emotions* to see what's really going on, take time to journal with them, and uncover their gifts.
- *Move your body every day,* either through exercise, stretching, or dance, to let energy move through you (after all, emotions are energy in motion).
- *Decide how you want to feel,* and make this choice on a regular basis, but not at the expense of emotions that surface organically.

When you gently and consciously—but not obsessively—look into and under your precious emotions, you are invited inside into a sacred place that is so richly *you*, a reservoir overflowing with precious jewels. You have nothing to fear here in your heart. Dive deep, and you will be rewarded for your courage, curiosity, and self-acceptance with wisdom and insight. Self-awareness is a wild kaleidoscope of colorful expressions within to be nourished.

When you take the time to nourish and become intimate and accepting of your inner emotional world, you'll reap the benefits that come with this level of healing, such as peace, contentment, and deep joy.

To discover the source of your emotions is to feel real connection and understanding. To accept your emotions is to accept yourself. To express your emotions is to allow yourself the fullness of life. Getting to know yourself through your emotions helps you feel tangibly more in touch with yourself. This will inevitably lead to a more abundant and accessible awareness.

When you learn the art of dancing with your emotions and courageously loving yourself the whole way, then the undercurrent of peace becomes stronger and joy is only a smile away.

· Practice ·
Sacred Self–Care Soul Prompts

Datebooks and diaries are practical portals into a more vibrant life full of self-care. It doesn't take long to plan your nourishment. Create space each day for the small acts of nourishment that you can do for yourself that make you happy and relaxed, and plan ahead for the bigger things, like appointments for massages, movie dates, nature hikes, and healing sessions. Make yourself your priority when planning ahead for your week and let your heart guide you toward the nourishment that's just right for you.

What self-care will you prioritize this week? Will you take yourself out for nature walks or book a massage? Will you take more breaks from work and social media? Will you begin a new ritual of self-care—such as self-massage or yoga—in the morning or evening?

What is your intention for this day, this month, and this year? How do you wish to feel today? How would you like the week ahead to look? What about the year ahead excites your Soul?

If you could write one affirmation that encapsulated your dreams for the month ahead, what would it be? How would you describe who you are becoming?

When was the last time you daydreamed? How does it feel for you to daydream? What do you dream about?

What emotions have been the strongest today? How did you feel, and how did you express and release them? How did you feel after you surrendered the heavy emotion?

Reach into Your Shadow

Every bright light casts a shadow; it's a natural part of being a shiny Soul. Everything in your shadow is simply a part of you that you've forgotten, repressed, hidden, or denied. You're not meant to deny any part of you, but you were inevitably taught to do so as a child. That's why it's so important to consciously embrace and understand your shadow as a real part of you. Without getting to know these aspects and giving them some air, they'll sit in the dark depths of your unconscious mind, corrupting your joy, impeding your growth, and tearing at your instinct's foundation. Knowing the deepest and darkest parts of you might feel strange at first, but these are some of the most important parts of you that require nourishment. If you don't nourish all of you, then you're hiding what you're ashamed of. Shame is a low-vibrating energy that will hinder you from ever reaching your full potential. Know and love all of you. It's as simple and as difficult as that.

The first step with shadow work is curiosity with the intention of loving healing. Entering the shadow with fear or denial won't help you on your path, so be sure to check in with your motivation before you dive deep. What you discover may cause your ego to flare up in the hope of blaming, judging, or getting angry at people who have caused you to deny parts of you or stay small. Go in with love; let the ego be quiet for a moment.

With a compassionate and honest heart, take out your journal and lay your emotions out in full. Without editing, judging, ignoring, or making up stories, take your time with the questions below. This is important work that will have beneficial and lasting effects throughout your entire life. Nourishing the shadow will cause your Soul to shine brighter than ever, create a more grounded and loving instinct, and put you more in touch with your intuitive heart. Anytime you sense your shadow self in everyday life, embrace whatever comes up for you and gently notice why negative emotions persist. Often, they're trying to heal your past and your instinct, for it is an unseen, camouflaged shadow that weighs down your instinctual response with fear. Take your time with this valuable work, and honor yourself for your strength and courage in stepping into and nourishing your shadow.

• PRACTICE •
Shadow Self Soul Prompts

Personally, I've discovered a lot about my shadow that wasn't at all as dark or traumatic as I thought it would be. Often, I simply heard my inner child quietly asking for a hug, for acknowledgment, or for reassurance that everything was okay. If the tears come, let them. Keep breathing deeply and let love into all the spaces of your being. You are completely safe here in your own transformation.

What feelings have been present lately that have made you uncomfortable? Where do you think they may have come from originally? What are they hoping to show you?

What parts of your personality do you consider unacceptable? What do you not like showing to other people? Where did the belief that these parts of you are shameful originate?

In what ways do you believe you are not good enough, worthy enough, or loveable enough? Where did these stories begin?

Whom do you need to forgive from your past? Write them a letter and safely burn it when you're finished. Let out all of your feelings, whether positive or negative, and be completely honest. Write until you feel a shift in your heart.

How is your inner child still afraid, lost, vulnerable, or sad? Write them a letter expressing how safe and loved they are. Tell them it's not their fault that difficulties occurred and reassure them that you'll sit with them as long as they need you. You may want to try this in a meditation. Imagine the adult, present-day version of you sitting with you as a child. Talk to your inner child and appreciate whatever response you receive. If you don't receive words from them, talk to them with reassuring words instead. Hug your inner child in your mind's eye and let them melt into your body with love.

Spend time freewriting or sitting in meditation as you ponder these questions. Allow messages from your shadow to flow without hesitation. Feel whatever you need to feel, allow it to pass through you, and when you're complete, give thanks. There are many spiritual coaches who can help you heal your shadow if you feel that you're not able to do this yourself.

Cherish Your Temple

Your inner wisdom is constantly giving you advice on all matters, great and small, especially on how to look after the temple of your body. Looking after bodies is big business. There are millions of teachers, healers, coaches, experts, gurus, trainers, and companies hoping that you'll give them your money, take their advice, buy their products, like their page, read their book, and follow their path. But you are the only one who knows what's good for your body.

You know what food and beverages truly benefit you. You know what exercise energizes, stretches, and heals. You know what self-care is imperative for your well-being. You know what kind of connection with nature you need. You know what health professionals have your best interest at heart. You know what beauty and skincare products are genuinely kind to your health and to Mother Earth. You know what conscious habits are worth making time for. You know what household products are natural and not draining your body's good health.

You know all of this because your inner wisdom has been telling you all along.

I used to feel uneasy using toxic makeup products, so I ditched them. I didn't get good vibes (or advice) from my old doctor, so I found a new one. I craved a fun range of exercise ideas to get my body moving, so I joined a gym for a year. I know how healing a bath is, so I make a decadent weekly ritual of it. I feel happiest at the beach, so I moved close to one.

I do what feels good and true for the sake of a long and happy life. And I'm not afraid to change my mind when I learn more, as I grow more, as my intuition becomes stronger, and when I need to pivot along my path.

If you're not sure what step to take, grab two options. Place them in front of you (or write them down if you need to) and tune in to each of them with your energy. Take note of how they make you feel. Honor that feeling and choose what feels expansive. One of them might start to sparkle, shine, pulsate, or give you tingles. The other one might feel awkward, uncomfortable, unsure, or constricted. If you don't get a clear answer, try the muscle testing process mentioned earlier in this book.

Be patient and purposeful in all that you do to take care of yourself. When you cultivate a strong knowing around what feels right for you and what doesn't, you'll carry this with you everywhere you go. This is the whole point of intuitive living—to hold on to this connection in the world and use it for your highest benefit.

*A few simple but often forgotten ideas
to kick-start a wave of body love:*

- Incorporate a soulful daily ritual into your morning shower, such as massaging your heart center in a clockwise motion with a gentle scrub, imagining the water to be healing white light filling you from your crown chakra, or humming a sweet tune to connect to your belly and lift your spirit.
- Use essential oils with warm jojoba oil to massage into your body post-shower.
- Stretch for a few minutes in the morning. Make up your own yoga practice or move your body in a way that feels good and easy.
- Lie belly to belly with Mother Earth and let her physically ground your body while balancing your emotions and spirit.
- Walk barefoot through sand, grass, dirt, or on rocks.
- Tell your body every day how much you love it and why. Be generous and specific.
- Purchase natural face and body products and bless them as you use them.
- Drink plenty of filtered water every day.
- Honor your body's true whole-food cravings.

When it comes to nourishment, your instinct is always guiding you away from what isn't best for you, your intuition is nudging you toward what is most aligned, and your insight is bringing in new ideas for holistic wellness that you may not have tried before. Stay open to the guidance.

Revive Your Energy

The energy in and around you will affect everything in your life, from your thoughts and emotions to your body, relationships, and level of vitality. Likewise, everything in your life may affect the energy in and around you.

It's up to you to create, nourish, and protect your precious energy and to only welcome in energy from others and your environment that is nourishing for you.

Energy is *everything*.

Our thoughts, emotions, words, and actions will greatly impact the energy in and around us. Even our densely physical body is pure energy. The energy that you influence in your field comes back to you in time—what you give, you receive. It's an energetic cycle that keeps on moving, changing, transforming, and affecting.

My favorite energetic quick fix is a meditation and a glass of water. No kidding. A ten-minute meditation in which I *ground* my instinctive/gut energy, *open* my heart/intuitive space, *clear* my third eye to gain valuable insight, and *connect* to Source is so completely healing to me. When I take time to visualize fluid alignment in my being, my energy responds to that positively and powerfully.

Ground, open, clear, and connect.

Your energy is in everything you do, and people will feel what you feel. When your heart is singing, expect compliments and random smiles. When you pour love into all you do, love comes back to hold you close. Believe in yourself and your purpose as your energy is enhanced by your beliefs, one way or another.

· RITUAL ·
Wild Energy Revivers

Here are a few ways to refresh your energy when you're feeling low, tired, or stuck. Quite often, it doesn't take much to turn your thoughts around, move your body, or try something new to shift your energy. Try these to see how they feel.

1. Meditate in the morning for five minutes, breathing deeply into your belly through your nose and completely out of your whole body through your nose or mouth. Do this without pausing; create a cyclical flow to your breathwork.

2. Set an intention each morning; choose a love-based, high-energy feeling that you would like to feel throughout your day. Write it down somewhere noticeable so that it can inspire you.

3. Set into place nonnegotiable ways of nurturing your physical energy each day, such as using essential oils, bending into yoga poses, sipping herbal teas, and choosing healthy snacks.

4. Say a little prayer for Great Spirit to stay close and shower you with miracles and clarity.

5. Hug a tree, dip your body in the ocean, or inhale a flower's beauty.

6. Look up at the sky for a few minutes and wonder with a smile at the mystery and cosmic wilderness of the universe.

As you heal yourself, you find yourself. Your inner wisdom cannot bloom if your energy is blocked, as instinctive, intuitive, and insightful wisdom is a continuous flow of *guidance as energy*.

Colorful Chakra Care

Chakras are a curious way of nourishing, healing, and understanding yourself better. When you're feeling out of balance and you can identify which chakra needs some self-care (either through the descriptions in chapter 3 or by meditating on your inner wisdom), try these ideas:

- Wear the specific chakra color on your clothes, accessories, or on something you're carrying; eat foods of a similar color or place matching crystals nearby.

- Say out loud the positive affirmations (provided with the chakra descriptions in chapter 3) that balance what's not working and reinforce what you want. For example, if you want to clear your throat chakra, try, "I express my truth every day with grace and clarity." If you want to open your crown chakra, say, "I am open to receiving wisdom and golden light from the highest dimensions." Say the affirmation consistently until you feel a shift.

- Lie down somewhere quiet and gently breathe into the chakra that needs healing, flooding the area with sparkly white light, feeling it enlarge and brighten with each breath until it is slightly wider than your body.

- Dance intuitively to music or do some intuitive flow yoga to allow healing energy to move through you. Wear and think of the color as you do so, or simply state an intention for healing to move through all chakras.

- Sit or lie down somewhere quiet with your eyes closed, imagining each chakra in your mind's eye or placing one hand over the area of your body where the chakra would be. Trust the insight you receive as you move slowly up each chakra from root to crown.

Nurturing Cycles and Inner Flow

Your cycles are a miraculous reflection of the cycles of the universe. Birth and death, fertility and creativity, love and loss, pain and ecstasy, sickness and healing, surrender and control. Your local community, the seasons, sunrise and sunset, moon cycles, stars, planets, and cosmic guides all have a cyclical nature to them. There are cycles within and around everything, guiding and governing, coming and going, moving and flowing according to divine timing and will.

Women and men both have remarkably potent cycles in their lives due to the currents of hormones in their bodies. Hormones fluctuate every hour, day, month, and season, putting us emotionally and energetically in touch with the seasons, elements, our local communities, our food, and the weather. Women bleed and ovulate once a month during their fertile years; they are the creators of the next generation—women who aren't mothers are still part of this, birthing, creating, and nurturing in countless ways. Women are also death's closest witness, as they make up the majority of midwives, nurses, and caretakers of the elderly.

Celebrating and honoring each internal and external cycle is a powerfully healing way to connect to Mother Earth, our bodies, and our inner wisdom. With honest acceptance and presence comes empowerment—to look after ourselves and our planet— and a deep-rooted sense of feeling and flow.

When you're eating imported food that doesn't align with the current season, you're blocking flow. When you're a bleeding woman or an exhausted man sweating it out at the gym, you're likely in pain or disconnected from your body, which will block flow. When you're forcing yourself to hustle when you genuinely need to rest, you're blocking the flow of healing.

When you tune in to the moon's energies and allow her to shine guidance on your rhythm, you find flow. When you honor what your body requires as it cycles through the day, you find flow. When you allow emotions to move like water, you find flow. When you nourish yourself in these ways and find flow, you'll feel the current of your intuition course within.

· RITUAL ·

Nourish Your Inner Cosmos

Here are some dynamic ways to love and learn more about the cosmos around and within you. Through these rituals, you will come to know your inner cycles more intimately, which is such an empowered way of living with self-awareness. Go with what intuitively feels good.

Keep a diary of your personal monthly cycle. Note how you feel each day, what foods you crave, what healing feels good, when your energy peaks, when you long for company, and when you need to rest solo. When you plan your life and business around your cycle, you will experience greater flow and ease. If you're a man or a woman who doesn't bleed, you'll still find deeper awareness and healing when you connect with how you feel throughout each month.

Connect with the moon. There are eight main rotations of the moon called lunar phases. Tune in to them intuitively or through a lunar calendar. Get inspired. Get curious. And most powerfully, get to know how *you* feel on each new and full moon. The moon is one of nature's great guides; she's there as a beacon for you to understand yourself better throughout each cycle.

Look to the stars. Astrology is a never-ending wonder of information and guidance. Each phase feels different and has many shades of guidance that come with it. Find an astrology calendar or website that you can observe, and, as always, make sure your own inner universe and feelings are the most important guidance for you, above what anyone else says about the stars.

Watch nature's unfolding. The seasons influence how you feel, what you eat, and what kind of movement you desire. When you attune your heart to nature's rhythm by spending time outside, by eating intuitively what your body is craving, by living in awe at the weather, by letting your body move as it wants to, you are in flow with nature and with the wildest parts of yourself.

Let go of expectations. When you expect things to be a particular way or have a specific outcome, you see the world as fixed and rigid when it's anything but. When you find peace within the highs and lows, pain and ecstasy, love and loss, when you cease clinging to the high ideals of perfection and accept *what is*, you align with flow and unearth the gifts of light tucked into the darkest and most unexpected moments.

Stay fluid with your creativity. Some days you may feel like the fullest, most inspired poet, artist, designer, architect, engineer, dancer, teacher, healer, or mystic. Other days you may feel empty, with nothing to give. This is the cycle of creativity. Do your best to create when you feel aligned to the source of your creativity and to rest and attend to other things when you feel the natural disconnect or pull-away. You simply cannot birth brilliance every single day.

See death as it truly is ... a transition, not an ending. For there is no *real* death. Your Soul—and the Soul of every living thing—lives forever. We birth, we grow, and we transition into a different form again and again. Such is the nature and wonder of our Soul's journey.

Divine timing is nonlinear, fluid, and flawless. Scheduling in earth time can be helpful, but all too often clock time can be seductive. The calendar year, your diary, alarm clocks, meetings, expectations, and appointments are all so appealing. When your life is ruled by the dictation of the ever-ticking clock, your inner cycle may be largely ignored because it doesn't "fit in" with the unnatural rhythm of clock time. When you move to the pulse of your body, you live in alignment with nature's cosmic and organic timing.

Wake with the sun. Rest with the night. Learn to say *no*. Be brave and say *yes* when your Soul is ready. Be as flexible as possible. Eat when you're hungry. Nap when you need to. Indulge in yourself and find your flow. Get to know yourself on this deeply intricate level. Get to love everything that you see. Nourish yourself in every imaginable way.

CREATING YOUR KIND OF COMMUNITY

You are the founder and foundation of *your* community. Creating a community of joy and support is more than just the loveliest feeling in the world, it's holistic and wholehearted nourishment all around you. But it all starts with you. You are the center of your web, and you get to weave it according to your inner rhythm and needs. Get to know your neighbors. Say hi to the people who work nearby. Offer your mail carrier cold water on a hot day. Wave to the kids who live in your street. Smile at strangers. Acknowledge the homeless. Volunteer at a local shelter or soup kitchen. Not for what they can give back to you, but for the simple nourishment that comes with looking after others.

There are no rules to connect with your community. Do it your way. Extend your heart outward from where you live in a way that feels nourishing, not depleting. Mostly, spread kindness.

We are all connected, especially when we live close to others. It doesn't mean you have to make contact with people who don't feel good. It doesn't mean you have to take criticism from people who are disrespectful. It just means that there are people out there who could benefit from your light. Connecting with a bunch of collective Souls that you can count on for various roles is a tangible way of growing roots. Even if you only live in one place for six months, having roots for a short period is nourishing for your adventurous energy.

There are many ways to reach out; choose the ways that light up your heart. Try a community class (learning or teaching), soulful circles, dog walking, visiting local fairs and garage sales, volunteering at schools, shopping at food markets, holding your own creative stall at a regular market, or looking after kids that live close by. Join or create a Facebook group where anyone can reach out and connect.

The more grounded, safe, and appreciated you feel in your hometown, the more secure your instinct will feel. A secure instinct creates space for a flourishing intuition, a powerful ability to receive insights, and a life of sublime self-awareness. When you feel supported by a group of locals who genuinely have your back, you move beyond surviving and start truly thriving. As you nourish others, you feel nourished yourself, even when you don't ask for anything in return. You matter to so many. When you realize this, your heartspace opens further and expands the energy around it, giving and receiving love and compassion every day. You also gain a grassroots element to your purpose, deepening a sense of meaning in every area of your life.

I've lived in nine areas of five different cities around the world, spreading roots into each of these communities. As a child, I didn't ever want to leave once I had made close friends, but moving countries a few times gave me faith that wherever I landed, I would be able to meet like-minded people and still keep in touch with those I had left behind.

This has been a huge blessing to me as I settle in my new hometown of Byron Bay. Although I miss my Sydney friends every day, I trust that this place is meant to be home for now. As we slowly cultivate a cherished and soulful community around us, we are mindful of bringing in people to our home and our hearts who feel aligned, and are committed to sharing our love and light openly with everyone we meet. Creating a conscious community is a circle of nourishment. Hugs when you need them, conversations that awaken you, meals for hard times, assistance with kids or pets, and the communal fire that burns bright for everyone.

Community is precious. Take care of yours.

HEALING FAMILY DYNAMICS

Families are complicated, unpredictable, messy, and completely unique to all of us. Each member of our family has the ability to impact our health in countless ways. I believe true nourishment must take into consideration all our relationships. Whether we rely on a family member too much for feelings of safety, security, or happiness, or if a family member is somehow causing us pain or unease, these are attachments that need to be let go of and connections that need healing.

Self-awareness means looking after ourselves in every way that our inner wisdom guides us to. It means paying attention to the relationships around us and noting honestly if they are nourishing or not. Creating space between yourself and a family member doesn't mean cutting them out of your life; it may mean having a difficult conversation with them to clear the energy between you, it could mean energy healing or visualization to heal old upsets or trauma, or it could mean disconnecting from them on social media and only connecting in real life when you feel ready to do so.

Family members teach us, inspire us, challenge us, and shape us in endless ways. Long ago when I started out on my personal path of self-awareness, I learned three things that shaped the way I see my family and helped me heal old wounds.

1. You choose your close family before you incarnate into a physical body.
2. Each family member has a task to do to help your Soul grow.
3. Your parents did the best job they knew how to with what they had.

We choose our family because we believe that they will give us the best chance at achieving what we want to achieve for our Soul. We don't choose to be abused or neglected—this is not our fault on any level, but we choose the people we are related to.

When I began to see my family as my greatest teachers, as the people who helped shape me—intentionally or otherwise—to be the beautiful person I am today, I took back my power and became grateful for my life and the family I am surrounded with. If I was ever to hold on to resentment, anger, jealousy, bitterness, guilt, or shame in relation to my childhood and family, then I would hold myself back from being completely nourished, healed, aware, and alive. A big part of nourishing my well-being is to forgive, love, and surrender who my family members are and all that they've done. They are so much more than their "wrongs." To hold on to negative feelings or attachments is to profoundly impede my health and the possibility of having a great relationship with them.

My family taught me to be an honest, independent, kind, intelligent, hilarious, creative, musical, hard-working, spiritual, and loving human being. Was it all easy? No. Am I perfect just the way I am today because of their devotion, love, integrity, sacrifice, generosity, and mistakes? Absolutely.

As a parent, I forgive myself more easily because I know I'm doing my best every day. Sometimes I yell. Sometimes I blame. Sometimes I eat their chocolate. But I'm healing, growing, and expanding my consciousness thanks to these children I've been blessed with. It's not easy creating, birthing, nourishing, raising, teaching, and loving a little human. It's wild. But if I can't nourish myself with the same devotion that I nourish my family with, I'm lacking in complete self-care.

However your family sits in your life right now, they are there because you called them in. They are there for a reason. Stop *trying* to forgive them and just forgive. You don't have to tell them, and it will free your heart. Don't spend time with people you don't want to be with just because they're family. Love them all anyway. Anything else will impact your health and well-being and get you stuck in a whirlpool of heartache. If you can, tell them you love them as often as possible.

Give up your attachments to all the members of your family. Let them be who they are. Don't expect anything from them. Gently peel your energy away from them until they don't impact your thoughts and emotions anymore. Get help to heal family issues and don't give yourself a hard time if it takes many therapy sessions and energy healings to feel the way you desire to feel. It's all necessary nourishment along your path.

If there's one way you can heal your family today, take a moment now or just before sleep to imagine all your family members together. Wrap them up in a soft pink, loving light. Send them all unconditional love, and feel the unconditional love come back to you from their Souls. Keep doing this until you feel the lightness of love all the way through your being.

Conscious Love

All your relationships need nourishing, especially your closest partnership. To love someone who understands and cherishes you for *all* of who you are is a blessing. Never let someone tear you down, abuse you, undermine you, rob you of your peace, or take you for granted. Walk away when your instinct urges you to do so. There is no shame in leaving.

Look after yourself first in any close relationship. Love yourself hard, and you will never beg for love for the rest of your days. Cherish yourself, tell yourself that you're beautiful every day, take yourself out for dates, and give yourself plenty of hugs. Nourish yourself wholeheartedly, because no one else can give you what you're not already accepting from yourself.

When you can fulfill your cravings on your own, you'll find the weight of your relationship so much lighter, and so will your partner. Of course, there will still be challenging and uncomfortable moments, as every partnership is about growth, but with self-care, you will bring a deeper level of empowerment and compassion to the union.

Embrace change and growth within yourself and your partner. Be patient with them, support them through their transformation, and love them unconditionally.

Love your body and let it be loved. Let your physical senses find pleasure every day. Relish your nakedness. Make love without shame or guilt, but rather with pure connectedness, consciousness, and curiosity. Laugh at the awkwardness that often accompanies sex and be honest about your feelings, pleasures, and boundaries.

When the going gets really tough, when arguments are more common than breakfast, when you cease to see their humanness as beautiful, consider whether a relationship counselor or energy healer would be of benefit.

Spend time alone. Revel in the beauty of your own presence. Use moments of stillness to open up to your intuition, and let the messages guide your relationship. When in doubt, ask yourself, *What would unconditional love do?*

NOURISH YOUR SPIRIT

Your unique spirit is the expression of your Soul, the lifeforce of your eternal self. Consciously tune in to your essence and energy daily, hourly, or as often as you can until you merge with this sensation and live from this place, until you are aligned with your true self in everything that you do. As you strive—with grace and ease—to live aligned, you will be one with your inner wisdom, one with Source energy, and one with your brothers and sisters, animals, and nature.

Breathwork is a powerful and pure way to feel and heal your body, your past, your traumas, and your emotions. Breathwork can be simple and blissful or intense and dynamic. There are many different types of therapeutic breathwork that you can learn online or from a practitioner—one-on-one or in a group—to consciously work with your unseen spirit. Your breath and spirit are vehicles to surrender, remedy, and salve the wholeness of you. And to bliss, always bliss.

As we complete this cycle of six steps, we come back full circle to the breath. Keep breathing deeply. Feel into your spirit through your breath each day.

Your spirit is exceptionally precious. Admire and nurture it accordingly.

Conclusion
and Appreciation

I'm wonderstruck and wildly grateful that you've completed this book, connected to it in your own way, and received what you needed. The integration of what you've learned may take some time, so go gently and really up-level the self-care as your self-awareness grows and you connect to your instinct, intuition, and insight daily.

Every deep *breath* is nourishment. Each one that you generously bring into your body gives you new life, fresh energy, more of the wild lifeforce. Every time you *surrender* is an act of epic courage. Each time you let go of what's not yours to carry, you create space to bloom. Every time you consciously *connect* to your inner self and the greater cosmos, you are deepening your intuitive experience of life. Every time you *trust* your inner wisdom as real and true, you send a wave of love and acknowledgment to your Soul. Every time you *honor* yourself by showing up in the world as your truth, you open up to the miracles of the universe. Every time you *nourish* yourself with healing love, you grow into your highest and most amazing potential. Stay gently aware of who you are and how you feel in each moment and how your heart is effortlessly leading you into the next.

Let love light the way.

· RITUAL ·
A Prayer for Your Soul's Voyage

My prayer for you on this journey is that you come to a place of peace amongst the chaos, love above fear, and authenticity no matter what.

I pray that you see yourself as your greatest, wisest, most divine guru. May you come to know your Soul intimately, reverently, and gratefully.

I pray with all my heart that somewhere in this book, you found your true nature—that you found love and softness and home all at once.

I pray that you devote your life from this day to the purpose that is written on your heart and in the light of your eyes. That you follow what you know is right for you, do what feels good, and fall into a graceful pace set by your Soul each and every day.

I pray that you know how deeply loved and guided toward joy you are by your Divine Team.

And I pray that you linger in a state of sweet serendipity and contented awareness often.

Take care and live true to your heart always.

Much love,
Kris

ACKNOWLEDGMENTS

Thank you, Great Spirit, Council of Light, Ancestors, Spirit Guides, and all beings of light who held, guided, and inspired me through the creation and birth of my first book. May every word honor your infinite Light and unconditional Love.

Mark, you are the most generous and brilliant person I know. Thank you for your unquestionable support and deep love. I love you completely and immeasurably. Lucas and Ariella, thank you for your patience when Mama was madly writing and editing. You two are my most precious portals of inspiration. I love you both beyond the multiverse and back.

I'm overwhelmed with love for my family—Mama, Dad, Steve, Pili, Audrey, Chris, Louise, Christel, and the extended bunch—for your endless support and love. You inspired my love of writing when I was small and stubborn (intuitive), created room for it to bloom, and have walked with me every step on this adventure. Thank you for the constant encouragement. I love you all so much.

Beáta Alföldi, for your empowerment, devotion, and love. You see the highest expression in everyone, and you go after it with your whole heart. Thank you for your healing and guidance.

Tom Cronin, for being a humble warrior of light. Thank you for holding space for me to find the deepest portal to nothing and everything all at once.

Theresa Voigt, thank you for being an unapologetic goddess of the highest vibrations. You make me laugh, you tend to my Soul, and you've brought endless peace and closure to my infinite being.

Troy Allan, for taking my hand and walking me through the quantum field, showing me the endless possibilities of healing, and saying yes to my wild ideas. Thank you for all that you do in service to our family and the world.

Jacqui Bushell, you are an earth angel, a Soul who radiates love to all the beings of the world like no one else I know. Thank you for the gift of Reiki, for opening this lightworker to a deeper understanding and love of the light.

Sarah McLeod, I am so blessed to know you, my Soul sister. Thank you for the life-changing healing you've brought to my life, and the way you wholeheartedly serve the world. The knowledge and healing of your heart is infinite.

Ashalyn, words cannot convey how deeply you shifted my life in two days on Shasta. I'm grateful to you for seeing through my doubt and stubbornness into my yearning heart and for connecting me with ancestors of long ago. Thank you.

Jodi Donovan, my sublime twin, you have opened me to the deepest and most beautiful expression of my truth by being honestly, hilariously, and humbly you. I adore you.

Anki Groening, thank you for freeing me from the captivity of my programmed creativity and showing me a new way to access my eternally creative heart. You rewilded me in all the right ways.

Lynda Osborne, my sister, I am so grateful every day for your eternal and expansive heart. You are such a joy and blessing to be around. Thank you for showing the world how to love.

Katrina Smith, thank you for your healing alchemy, our deeply insightful conversations, and our cherished connection. I'm blessed to be walking this path with you by my side.

Keri Krieger, your real and raw support has always been close by. Thank you for our connection, full of shared earth wisdom and the wildest laughter. You are a total goddess.

Danielle Minogue, you came into my life at the most sublime time and have taught me so much about grace, humility, and presence. Thank you for our incredible friendship, my sister. You are a container for divine love like no other.

To the hearts that poured their personal stories into this book, thank you. Ros Scott-Mackenzie, you are a true inspiration and gifted healer. Lu Purvis, my Lemurian light, I'm grateful for our two lives together in this one. Jarka Kunova, my mentor, friend, and the greatest cheerleader, I appreciate our Soul connection. Jodie Matthews, your love and light radiate beyond words; thank you for stepping into your gift wholeheartedly. Erin Williams, you are an angel of kindness, my sweet friend. Hanna, you inspire me endlessly with your unapologetic luminosity. Satyam, you unknowingly planted a seed of light that I am deeply grateful for.

Kirra Smith, you generous minx, thank you for your gift. No matter where you go, sunbeams find you on your path. Thank you for bringing so much light onto mine.

The Collective Heart (Donna, Sascha and Hana), thank you for humoring, supporting, celebrating, and inspiring me endlessly. I adore you three like a deer loves flowers.

The incredible team at Llewellyn—you are all such wise and talented beings for whom I'm endlessly grateful. Angela Wix, your belief in this impassioned idea of mine was evident from the start, and your inspiration and direction shaped this book for the better. Sami Sherratt, thank you for your magical eye for detail and helping me take this message to the next level. Shira Atakpu, one day I hope to hug you so hard with the most heartfelt gratitude for designing the cover of this book. It is perfect and stunning in every way. Thank you. Mary Ann Zapalac, so much gratitude for adding the most divine touches to these pages. I'm blessed to work with all of you to bring this vision to life. Thank you to everyone who played an important role in publishing this book. I'm humbled by your belief and brilliance.

To my clients all over the world, I'm overjoyed to be of service in any way that has brought you home to yourself, to love, and to your purpose. Thank you for inspiring parts of this book by sharing your heart honestly with mine.

Finally, thank you, sweet reader. This was all for you. Stay wild.

Bibliography

Barnum, Melanie. *The Book of Psychic Symbols: Interpreting Intuitive Messages.* Woodbury, MN: Llewellyn, 2018.

Boland, Yasmin. *Moonology: Working with the Magic of Lunar Cycles.* London: Hay House, 2016.

Campbell, Joseph. *The Power of Myth.* New York: Anchor, 1991.

Dale, Cindi. *The Complete Book of Chakra Healing: Activate the Transformative Power of Your Energy Centers.* St. Paul, MN: Llewellyn, 1996.

Fairchild, Alana. *Crystals Angels 444: Healing with the Divine Power of Heaven and Earth.* Victoria, AU: Blue Angel, 2013.

Freud, Sigmund. *The Unconscious.* London: Penguin, 2005.

Hawkins, David R. *Letting Go: The Pathway to Surrender.* Carlsbad, CA: Hay House, 2012.

Hawks, S., H. Madanat, J. Hawks, and A. Harris. "The Relationship between Intuitive Eating and Health Indicators among College Women." *American Journal of Health Education* 36, no. 6 (November–December 2005): 331–336. https://doi.org/10.1080/19325037.2005.10608206.

Hetherington, Michael. *The Art of Self Muscle Testing: For Health, Life and Enlightenment.* Brisbane, AU: CreateSpace, 2013.

Hodgkinson, G. P., J. Langan-Fox, and E. Sadler-Smith. "Intuition: A fundamental bridging construct in the behavioural sciences." *British Journal of Psychology* 99, no. 1 (2008): 1–27. https://doi .org/10.1348/000712607X216666.

Jung, Carl. *Synchronicity: An Acausal Connecting Principle.* Princeton, NJ: Princeton University Press, 2010.

Kounios, J., and M. Beeman. "The *Aha!* Moment: The Cognitive Neuroscience of Insight." *Current Directions in Psychological Science* 18, no. 4 (August 2009): 210–216. https://doi.org/10.1111 /j.1467-8721.2009.01638.x.

Maniscalco, J. W., and L. Rinaman. "Vagal Interoceptive Modulation of Motivated Behavior." *Physiology* 33, no. 2 (March 2018): 151–167: https://doi.org/10.1152/physiol.00036.2017.

McCraty, R. *The Energetic Heart: Bioelectromagnetic Interactions Within and Between People.* New York: Marcel Dekker, 2004. https://www.heartmath.org/research/research-library /energetics/energetic-heart-bioelectromagnetic-communication -within-and-between-people/.

———. *Science of the Heart: Exploring the Role of the Heart in Human Performance.* HeartMath, 2015. https://store.heartmath.org /health-practitioners-books/science-of-the-heart.html.

McCraty, R., M. Atkinson, and R. T. Bradley. "Electrophysiological Evidence of Intuition: Part 1. The Surprising Role of the Heart." *The Journal of Alternative and Complementary Medicine* 10, no. 1 (2004): 133–143. https://doi.org/10.1089/107555304322849057.

Napthali, Sarah. *Buddhism for Mothers: A Calm Approach to Caring for Yourself and Your Children.* NSW, AU: Allen & Unwin, 2010.

Newtown, Michael. *Destiny of Souls: New Case Studies of Life Between Lives.* Woodbury, MN: Llewellyn, 2014.

Tribole, Evelyn, and Elyse Resch. *Intuitive Eating: A Revolutionary Program That Works.* New York: St Martin's Press, 1995.

Ware, Bronnie. *The Top Five Regrets of the Dying: A Life Transformed by the Dearly Departing.* Carlsbad, CA: Hay House, 2012.

Williams, Alice. *Bad Yogi: The Funniest Self-Help Memoir You'll Ever Read.* Victoria, AU: Affirm Press, 2018.

RECOMMENDED RESOURCES

Archetypes: www.archetypes.com

Ascended Masters: www.ascendedmasterindex.com

Ask Angels: www.ask-angels.com/archangels

Chakras: www.chakras.info

Decluttering Inspiration: www.konmari.com

Emotional freedom technique (EFT): www.thetappingsolution.com

EMDR: www.emdr.com

HeartMath Institute: www.heartmath.com

Insight Timer: www.insighttimer.com

Mental Health Help: www.beyondblue.org.au

Scientific Insights: www.sciencedaily.com

Spotify: www.spotify.com

Psychology of Intuition: www.psychologytoday.com

INDEX

A

Abundance, 9, 26, 36, 48, 57, 70, 87, 92, 97, 103, 170, 192, 193

Affirmations, 48–52, 71, 81, 108, 113–115, 156, 169, 193, 197, 198, 202, 210

Alignment, 3, 9, 12, 14, 16, 18, 19, 34, 36, 40, 45, 46, 53–55, 58, 68, 89, 119, 153, 190, 208, 214

Altar, 103, 170

Ancestors, 3, 20, 28, 48, 103, 116, 135, 145, 179, 193, 225, 226

Angels, 5, 38, 41, 135, 138–143, 145, 146, 151, 156, 158, 166, 174, 185, 226, 227

Anxiety, 65, 73, 90, 95, 97–99

Archangels (*see* Angels)

Art, 77, 90, 103, 104, 141, 142, 169, 202

Ascended Masters, 137, 146, 156, 158

Attachments, 33, 35, 49, 70, 74, 77–81, 84, 86, 89, 90, 118, 216, 218

Automatic writing, 22

Awakening, 68–70, 74, 142, 154, 173

B

Biology, 123, 124

Brain, 2, 4, 20, 21, 23–25, 29, 31, 34, 35, 39–41, 45, 62, 64, 92, 113–115, 128, 186

Breath, 1, 6, 17, 23, 34, 38, 53, 54, 59, 62–69, 71–75, 77, 79, 92, 94, 96, 100, 102, 107, 111, 115, 118, 120, 134, 154, 174, 177, 180, 183, 210, 220, 221, 223

C

Chakras, 2, 3, 46–53, 105, 106, 138, 153, 167, 196, 207, 210

Communion, 12, 16, 45, 68, 111, 120, 173

Community, 37, 60, 105, 132, 171, 172, 196, 211, 214–216

Connection, 2, 4, 6, 7, 11, 12, 16, 24, 29, 32, 33, 36, 40, 48, 52, 54, 55, 58, 69, 70, 101, 103, 111–113, 115, 116, 121, 123–125, 131, 133, 136–138, 142, 143, 145, 151, 155, 168, 170, 171, 175, 176, 180, 184, 195, 197, 202, 206, 207, 216, 226, 227

Conscious mind, 21, 29–31, 39, 40

Consciousness, 16, 21, 39, 52, 53, 116, 125, 127, 137, 176, 218, 220

Craving, 3, 60, 80, 123, 125, 141, 168, 185, 196, 207, 213, 219

Creativity, 11, 29, 38, 39, 49, 66, 92, 133, 135, 142, 189, 193, 198, 211, 213, 226

Crystals, 9, 26, 69, 80, 103, 127, 156, 158, 177, 210

Cycles, 1, 46, 63, 68, 127, 129, 172, 196, 208, 211–214, 221

D

Daydream (*see* Dream)

Decluttering, 89, 90

Depression, 90, 95, 97, 99

Divine Team, 135, 136, 138, 149, 158, 179, 224

Dream, 6, 12, 30, 40, 74, 80, 92, 107, 120, 133, 139, 140, 147, 152, 169, 173, 180–184, 188–190, 198, 199, 202, 203

E

Ego, 13, 15, 22, 26, 32, 33, 40, 68, 72, 78, 80, 81, 88, 89, 95–97, 100, 116–120, 125, 167–169, 173, 180, 182, 186, 203

Electromagnetic field (EMF), 27, 34, 35

Emotions, 7, 16, 22, 26, 29, 30, 34–39, 42, 49, 53, 73, 74, 77, 92, 93, 95, 98, 99, 103, 114, 116, 118, 119, 121, 123, 125, 126, 129, 149, 155, 173, 183, 194, 196, 199–204, 207, 208, 212, 218, 220

Empath, 42

Energy healing, 52, 70, 185, 186, 217, 218

Energy vortex, 161

Exercise, 7, 12, 22, 28, 57, 65, 66, 131, 173, 196, 201, 206

Eye movement desensitization and reprocessing (EMDR), 23

F

Family (*see* Relationships)

Fear, 15, 20, 25, 29, 32, 48, 63, 65, 70–74, 77, 80, 81, 91, 96, 97, 102, 104, 107, 112, 115–118, 125, 131, 135, 141, 142, 164, 171, 175, 180, 182, 190, 196, 197, 201, 203, 204, 224

Food, 24, 26–28, 36, 69, 80, 81, 84, 89, 90, 92, 122–127, 130–132, 137, 168, 182, 185, 187–189, 192, 206, 210–212, 215

Friendship, 28, 67, 139, 148, 157, 162, 165, 170, 171, 173, 187, 220, 226, 227

G

Gratitude, 8, 12, 14, 43, 49, 71, 75, 83, 84, 86, 101, 130, 136, 137, 145, 147, 154, 158, 173, 191, 193, 197, 227, 228

Great Spirit, 13, 25, 29, 38, 41, 44, 48, 52, 54, 60, 61, 82, 83, 88, 102, 106, 111, 116, 126, 127, 138, 139, 149, 155, 156, 169, 177, 202, 208, 209, 213, 220, 225

Grounding, 21, 48, 57, 65, 68, 69, 129

H

Heart, 1, 2, 4–7, 13, 14, 18–21, 23, 29, 34–40, 45, 48, 50, 51, 54, 57–61, 64, 65, 69–71, 73, 75, 77, 78, 81, 83–85, 90–93, 96, 97, 101, 103, 105, 107, 109, 112, 114–116, 118–120, 125, 128, 129, 131, 133–135, 137, 140, 147, 149–152, 155–158, 162, 164–166, 168–174, 177, 179–184, 187, 189, 191, 193, 196, 198–208, 213, 215, 216, 218, 223–228

HeartMath Institute, 34, 35

Highest Self, 14, 22, 33, 42, 52, 58, 70, 84, 95, 102, 104, 107, 112, 113, 117, 120, 129, 137, 146, 159, 176, 180, 181

Homeopathy, 86, 90, 185

Honor, 2, 5, 6, 14, 30, 32, 36, 50, 58, 67, 81, 101, 103, 117, 158, 170, 172, 179–187, 189–195, 197, 198, 204, 206, 207, 212, 223, 225

Hormones, 34, 211

I

Inner senses, 3, 31, 41, 43, 54, 106, 146, 153–155

Insight, 1–6, 9, 11–13, 19, 31, 38–46, 48, 51–53, 57, 58, 61, 62, 66, 67, 91, 107, 112–114, 129, 136, 139, 141, 142, 148–150, 153–157, 164, 180, 182, 193, 200, 201, 207, 208, 210, 215, 223

Instinct, 1, 2, 4, 5, 9, 11, 12, 19–29, 33, 45, 46, 48–50, 57, 58, 62, 66, 115, 116, 129, 136, 148, 164, 167, 203, 204, 207, 215, 219, 223

Intention, 28, 103, 104, 137, 138, 142, 145, 154, 155, 158, 159, 172, 176, 183, 184, 196–198, 202, 203, 209, 210

Intuition, 1, 2, 4, 5, 9, 11–13, 19, 28–35, 37, 45, 46, 48, 50–52, 57, 58, 62, 65, 78, 88, 103, 104, 109, 114, 115, 117, 121, 122, 125–127, 134, 136, 148–151, 154, 156, 157, 163–166, 172, 175, 179, 180, 182, 189–191, 195, 206, 207, 212, 215, 220, 223

J

Journaling, 12, 15, 16, 22, 107, 143, 184, 193

L

Lifeforce, 1, 6, 36, 59, 62, 69, 71, 75, 123, 180, 220, 223

Limbic brain, 29, 114

Love, 4, 7, 11, 13, 14, 17, 20, 22, 25, 26, 29, 32, 34, 36, 40, 44, 46, 48, 50, 51, 53, 54, 58, 60, 63, 66, 70–75, 81, 82, 84, 87–89, 94–99, 101, 102, 104–107, 111–113, 115–119, 123–126, 128, 131, 132, 134–140, 142, 144–146, 149, 152, 158, 162, 163, 165–167, 169–171, 173, 180, 181, 183, 188, 190–193, 195–198, 201, 203–205, 207, 208, 211–220, 223–228

Loved Ones, 3, 38, 41, 143–146, 149

M

Meditation, 3, 7, 12, 15, 22, 23, 37, 42, 43, 46, 53, 55, 66, 68, 69, 71, 102, 105, 107, 112–116, 128, 136, 138, 139, 142–145, 147, 151, 154, 155, 165, 173, 205, 208

Mindfulness, 16, 95–100, 108, 112, 199

Miscarriage, 86, 130

Motherhood, 86, 99

Mother Nature (*see* Nature)

Muscle testing, 175, 177, 206

N

Nature, 3, 5, 26, 28, 30, 32, 36–38, 42, 48, 54, 60, 65, 67–69, 95, 102, 112, 115, 122, 127–130, 132, 134, 135, 137, 144–146, 148, 152, 156, 162, 165, 174, 182, 194, 202, 206, 211–214, 220, 224

Naturopath, 98, 130

Neocortex, 29, 39, 40, 112

Neuro-emotional technique (NET), 23

Nourish, 6, 12, 19, 22, 25, 27, 53, 58, 81, 83, 112, 131, 167, 173, 195, 201, 203, 208, 212, 214, 215, 218–220, 223

O

Oracle cards, 103, 136, 156, 157, 174

P

Panic attacks, 85

Parasympathetic nervous system, 23

Pauses, 66, 67, 96, 101, 125, 126, 152, 174

Physical senses, 29–31, 34, 37, 41, 120, 121, 219

Pleasure, 32, 33, 49, 62, 126, 127, 133, 137, 219, 220

Pregnancy, 141, 172

Presence, 1, 12, 25, 26, 34, 39, 40, 54, 61, 66, 75, 80, 81, 83–85, 89, 135, 138, 140–145, 147, 148, 151, 163, 173, 191, 211, 220, 227

Protection, 11, 101, 102, 104–106, 140, 141

Psychic abilities, 43, 51, 67

Purpose, 3, 5, 26, 37, 44, 48, 52, 57, 68, 82, 87, 92, 104, 133, 134, 137, 141, 142, 163, 170, 179, 181, 182, 186–191, 208, 216, 224, 228

R

Reiki healing (*see* Energy healing)

Relationships, 6, 12, 15, 16, 20, 21, 26, 28, 48, 50, 60, 94, 98, 116, 124, 136, 140, 142, 143, 165, 167, 171, 175, 182, 185, 186, 190, 192, 208, 216–220, 225, 226

Reptilian brain, 20, 29, 39, 115

Rituals, 6, 18, 53, 57, 58, 65, 67, 71, 74, 81, 83, 95, 101–106, 108, 109, 112, 114, 115, 128, 138, 142, 145, 154, 169, 175, 183, 193, 196–198, 202, 206, 207, 209, 212, 224

S

Self-care/love, 14–16, 50, 61, 86, 91, 100, 114, 172, 174, 180, 183, 196–198, 202, 206, 210, 218, 219, 223

Sensitivities, 112, 129–131, 191, 192

Serendipity, 6, 15, 17, 53, 146, 152, 165, 184, 224

Shadow, 3, 22, 23, 25, 26, 112, 183, 203–205

Shamanic, 2, 23

Signs, 70, 113, 137–139, 141, 144–147, 150, 152, 183

Sisters / sisterhood (*see* Friendship)

Soul, 1–3, 7–9, 14–17, 22, 25–27, 32, 33, 35, 37, 41, 43–45, 52–54, 59–61, 63, 64, 67–75, 78–83, 86–89, 93–97, 100–103, 105–107, 109, 113, 116, 117, 119, 120, 126, 128, 131, 134, 137, 143, 148, 150, 152, 153, 157, 158, 161, 164–166, 168–170, 173, 175, 180–187, 190–193, 199, 202–204, 214, 215, 217, 219, 220, 223, 224, 226, 227

Source (*see* Great Spirit)

Spirit, 2, 3, 5, 9, 12, 19, 25, 26, 28, 29, 36, 38, 39, 41–45, 52–54, 58, 60–63, 68, 69, 81–83, 88, 100–102, 105, 106, 111–113, 116, 119, 127, 131, 133, 135–139, 143–146, 149, 151, 153–159, 162, 163, 169, 173, 174, 176, 179, 181, 183, 188, 190, 207, 209, 220, 221, 225

Spirit Guides, 38, 41, 105, 136–138, 143–146, 149, 151, 158, 174, 176, 225

Spiritual, 2, 3, 5, 11, 25, 39, 41–44, 47, 55, 60–62, 70, 72, 78, 82, 87–89, 95, 124, 130, 133, 135, 141, 147, 149–151, 155, 156, 176, 179, 182, 186, 189, 196, 205, 218

Stillness, 75, 81, 91, 93, 95, 96, 101, 147, 220

Stress, 24, 27, 64, 65, 73, 91, 128, 184

Subconscious mind, 21, 29–31, 33

Surrender, 2, 6, 52, 54, 58, 68, 77–84, 88, 89, 91, 93–109, 113, 115, 150, 151, 153, 174, 180, 195, 200, 211, 217, 220, 223

Symbols, 113, 138, 139, 145–147, 151, 152

Sympathetic nervous system, 23, 64

Synchronicity, 15, 146, 150, 177, 194

T

Toxins, 130

Trust, 2, 5–7, 12, 17, 30, 36, 41, 42, 45, 49, 51, 52, 58, 70, 83, 105, 107, 113, 115, 120, 127, 137, 138, 140, 142–146, 149, 150, 155, 159, 161–177, 179, 180, 187, 189, 195, 210, 216, 223

U

Unconscious mind, 19, 21, 22, 26, 30, 174, 203

Universe, 1, 4, 8, 13, 39, 41, 45, 46, 71, 87, 88, 91, 93, 108, 111, 115, 116, 120, 127, 146, 151, 172–174, 176, 188, 189, 194, 199, 209, 211, 213, 223

V

Vagus nerve, 23–25, 63, 64, 120

STAY CONNECTED

I'd love to support you on your intuitive journey.

Intuitive Living Meditations. For access to meditations that bring you closer to your heart: www.krisfranken.com/meditations.

Spiritual Courses. Discover self-led online courses to help you create deeper meditations, healing, and rituals in your life: www.krisfranken.com/courses.

Soul Purpose Mentorship Program. To work with me personally and find deeper alignment with your path and purpose: www.krisfranken.com/mentoring.

Oracle Cards. Surround yourself with abundance, beauty, and positivity with these oracle cards: www.krisfranken.com/shop.

Conscious Healing Retreats. Join me on healing retreats around the world: www.krisfranken.com/retreats.

Sacred Sunday Community. Receive a monthly letter and be the first to know about my offerings and giveaways: https://bit.ly/2YL8UUj.

For further information about this book: www.krisfranken.com/thecallofintuition.

Facebook: kris.franken

Instagram: @kris_franken

Pinterest: @kris_franken

TO WRITE TO THE AUTHOR

If you wish to contact the author or would like more information about this book, please write to the author in care of Llewellyn Worldwide Ltd. and we will forward your request. Both the author and the publisher appreciate hearing from you and learning of your enjoyment of this book and how it has helped you. Llewellyn Worldwide Ltd. cannot guarantee that every letter written to the author can be answered, but all will be forwarded. Please write to:

Kris Franken
⅟ Llewellyn Worldwide
2143 Wooddale Drive
Woodbury, MN 55125-2989

Please enclose a self-addressed stamped envelope for reply,
or $1.00 to cover costs. If outside the U.S.A., enclose
an international postal reply coupon.

Many of Llewellyn's authors have websites with additional information and resources. For more information, please visit our website at http://www.llewellyn.com.